SABBATH REST

Is there something missing in your busy life?

by

Kevin Morgan

TEACH Services, Inc.
Brushton, New York

2002 03 04 05 06 07 08 09 10 11 · 5 4 3 2 1

The author assumes full responsibility for the accuracy of all facts and quotations as cited in this book.

Copyright © 2002 TEACH Services, Inc.
ISBN 1-57258-230-8
Library of Congress Catalog Card No. 2002104147

Published by

TEACH Services, Inc.
www.tsibooks.com

Dedication

*S*abbath Rest is dedicated to all sincere seekers
of truth who are desperate to take a "spiritual
breather" from the hectic grind of modern life

in memory of
Dr. Calvin L. Thrash,

a dear friend whose desire for truth led Him to
Jesus' Sabbath rest and who is now resting in
Jesus until the morning of the resurrection.

Table of Contents

Acknowledgments

Without the many friends and colleagues who have supported me throughout the process of turning the results of several years of biblical and historical research into a readable book, you would not be holding this invitation to God's *Sabbath Rest*.

Of these individuals, I particularly want to thank Sean Wheeler, lover of truth and evangelist-in-training with *Amazing Facts,* who read an earlier form of this book and encouraged me to get the material into print. I also want to thank my mother, Doris Morgan, who, in the early days of my research, acted as my "book distributor," sharing copies of the manuscript with other interested parties.

Special thanks are also due to Dr. Jack Blanco for his invaluable suggestions in the order and content of several sections of the book and to Luke Miller, whose artistic eye guided in the design of the book's cover. Many thanks are also in order to the members of the churches in North and South Carolina who have permitted me to work out the logic of this book in their pulpits. And, to the audience who has been the most supportive of me throughout this book's development—my wife, Susan, and our children, Rebekah, Sharon, Adam, Ada, and Emily, I can only say, thanks for sticking with me through the countless modifications of the book. *It is finally finished!*

More than to any other, I want to express my deepest gratitude to the Lord Jesus Christ for giving us the gifts of *life, salvation* and *the Sabbath,* the last of which (though of lesser importance than the first two) reminds us that we are doubly His—once because He made us and twice because He redeemed us back from sin (*Mark 2:27; Exodus 20:8–11; Hebrews 4:9; Deuteronomy 5:12–15*).

—Pastor Kevin Morgan
Honor Him Min@cs.com

1

It's time that we take time for God.

*L*ike other Americans, have you found yourself recently rethinking your priorities? Perhaps you—like many others—have started thinking about taking more time to appreciate *life* and *family* and *God*.

It was far too easy to take these things for granted until—suddenly and without warning—the violent attacks of September 11th jarred our American senses into the realization that "business as usual" can no longer be the order of the day. As the smoke of the collapsed buildings has cleared and the shock, anger, sadness, and fear have subsided, we have, with sobered reflection, contemplated the suggestion that these unthinkable events may actually provide us with an opportunity to realign our priorities. For, though we may have succeeded in building impressive monuments to human ability, we have not succeeded in constructing our lives, our families, and our society upon values that will endure into eternity. Signs on many churches across this land have echoed the refrain:

"AMERICA, IT'S TIME TO PRAY."

"AMERICA, IT'S TIME TO GET BACK TO GOD."

Of course, it shouldn't require a crisis for us to take time for God. The Heavenly Father, who comforts and sustains in times of distress, is always ready to hear the prayers of His children and has issued, in the heart of the ten commandments, a standing invitation for every man, woman, and child to come apart from all the busyness of their lives and take time with Him, finding strength for their weekly challenges.

> *"Remember the sabbath day, to keep it holy. [9] Six days shalt thou labour, and do all thy work: [10] But the seventh day is the sabbath of the LORD thy God: in it thou shalt not do any work, thou, nor thy son, nor thy daughter, thy manservant, nor thy maidservant, nor thy cattle, nor thy stranger that is within thy gates: [11] For in six days the LORD made heaven and earth, the sea, and all that in them is, and rested the seventh day: wherefore the LORD blessed the sabbath day, and hallowed it."*
> *Exodus 20:8–11.*

This invitation to take special, weekly time (or *Sabbath rest)* with God has been echoed of late by a flurry of books* and by the appeals of various religious leaders.

Religious leaders call for Sabbath revival.

With his recent pastoral letter calling for greater faithfulness in Sunday church attendance, Pope John Paul II (with the support of others) has brought *Sabbath rest* into the public arena.

> "The theme of 'God's rest' (cf. Gn 2:2) and the rest which he offered to the people of the Exodus when they entered the Promised Land (cf. Ex 33:14; Dt 3:20; 12:9; Jos 21:44; Ps 95:11) is re-read in the New Testament in the light of the definitive '*Sabbath rest*' (Heb 4:9) . . . It is crucially important that all the faithful should be convinced that they cannot live their faith . . . unless they take part in the Sunday Eucharistic assembly. . . ." —Pope John Paul II, *Dies Domini,* May 1998, *emphasis supplied.*

> "In this country, Sunday has fallen by the wayside and Christians need to recover its sacred character." —David Phillips, director of the Church Society, Church of England.

> "God wrote the Sabbath into the very order of things. He said things would go better if you observe it." —Jack Lowndes, president of the Lord's Day Alliance.

---

* Examples include: *Sabbath: Restoring the Sacred Rhythm of Rest* by Wayne Muller, *The Sabbath* by Abraham Joshua Heschel, *Keeping the Sabbath Wholly* by Marva J. Dawn, *Celebrating the Sabbath: Finding Rest in a Restless World* by Bruce A. Ray, *The Sabbath: Entering God's Rest* by Barry & Steffi Rubin, *Sabbath Sense: a Spiritual Antidote for the Overworked* by Donna Schaper, *Sabbath Time* by Tilden Edwards, and *Catch Your Breath: God's Invitation to Sabbath Rest* by Don Postema.

In our modern, technologically advanced and commercially-centered world, a day set aside for rest and worship may seem a bit old-fashioned and impractical, yet we have found that technology has not been able to fix our most perplexing modern social problems and an abundance of material goods has not brought us real happiness.

Moreover, while the evolutionary scientific establishment of *modernism* may have taken it for granted that human life came about—without God—by chance, today many other thoughtful scientists are beginning to give the concepts of purposeful creation and a Creator God a second look. (After all, how does chance explain our love for beauty, order, or compassion?) Today, *post*-modern man has begun to look beyond the confines of science and materialism for meaning. Yet his search has not always led him to the one true God, for he has frequently been sidetracked by the lure of impersonal pantheistic power, by the promise of a direct, mystical connection with supernatural forces which bypass reason, or by the seductive appeal of the "gods" of his own making, created in the image of his own subjective truth.

The Creator God revealed

But the Creator is not to be found in the subjectivity of one's own experience. He is not the product of superstition or human imagination. He is not merely a force in nature, but is the One who created nature, as we find in the opening chapter of the Bible.

"In the beginning God created the heavens and the earth."
Genesis 1:1.

On the successive days of the creation week, God brought into existence everything which makes up the natural world: light, earth's atmosphere, dry land and plant life, the celestial lights, and the creatures of air, sea and land. On the sixth day of that week, as the crowning act of His creation, God made humankind. Then, because He knew how important it was for human beings to remember the One who created them and who alone can satisfy the inner longings of the human soul, He set aside a special day, as a memorial of His creatorship.

"Thus the heavens and the earth were finished, and all the host of them. ² And on the seventh day God ended his work which he had made; and he rested on the seventh day from all his work which he had made. ³ And God blessed the seventh day, and sanctified it: because that in it he had rested from all his work which God created and made." Genesis 2:1–3.

The Sabbath was made for man.

What God "made" on the seventh day of the creation week was very different from anything that He had made on any of the previous days of creation. He *made time* to spend with his children—a gift that every child wants from his or her father.

". . . The Sabbath was made for man . . ." Mark 2:27.

When God "rested . . . and blessed . . . and sanctified" the seventh day, He made a standing appointment with mankind. He put aside the commodity that post-modern man currently needs most—time for *rest* and for *reflection.*

The Sabbath tells us who God created us to be.

Contrary to the dictates of society and industry which would have us all work every day of the week like *robots* or *beasts of burden,* God wanted us to have the weekly Sabbath experience to help us remember what He created us to be—*human beings, created in the image of a loving Father (Genesis 1:26).*

"God so loved the world that He gave us the Sabbath. . . . Sabbath, from the Hebrew, *Shabbat,* means very simply 'rest.' He gave us a day of rest. When everybody else—from the taskmasters of the Pharaoh . . . to the slave owners of the South . . . were saying, 'Work! Lift! Push! Haul!' God says: 'Rest, my Son. Rest, my daughter.'" —D. James Kennedy, "The Gift of Rest," *Coral Ridge Hour,* November 4, 2001.

Because He knew how easy it would be for busy modern man to forget Him (and to forget who God created him to be), God Himself has issued to our generation—within the final pages of the symbolic book of Revelation—a clarion call to return to Him in worship:

"And I saw another angel fly in the midst of heaven, having the everlasting gospel to preach unto them that dwell on the earth, and to every nation, and kindred, and tongue, and people, 7 saying with a loud voice, Fear God, and give glory to him; for the hour of his judgment is come: and worship Him who made heaven, and earth, and the sea, and the fountains of waters." Revelation 14:6, 7.

"Sunday bests" with no *Sabbath rest*

Today, many people are turning again to the worship of the Creator, through the traditional Sunday morning worship hour of their parents and grandparents. Yet, as refreshing as this trend may be, the "Sunday morning worship hour" is still not Sabbath rest. It does not represent a total break from the weekly grind. When church is over, off come the "Sunday bests" and the rest of the day, with all its many activities, is just about as busy as any other. The "rest" of the day has no rest.

"We think that we're doing him a big favor if we show up at church on Sunday morning, or maybe even Saturday night, and then we figure, 'Good, I've taken care of that obligation. Now I can do whatever I want.' I think so much of the difficulties, the hardship, the tension, and the anxieties that we read about and hear about in the news every day is a result of the fact that people never get time to deflate." —George Barna, "Remember the Sabbath?" www.cbn.org.

The Sabbath reminds us of who God is.

As the memorial and reminder of God's rest on the seventh day of Creation, the Sabbath was observed by both Jews and Christians on the seventh day of the week—the day we now call *Saturday*. (It was only with the gradual abandonment of the biblical seventh-day Sabbath that Sunday morning services came into being and were bequeathed as a legacy to our present generation.) Keeping the seventh day reminds us of what God has done.

"For he spake in a certain place of the seventh day on this wise, And God did rest the seventh day from all his works." Hebrews 4:4.

Steffi, a friend of my family, who comes from a Buddhist background and who married a young man who keeps the Sabbath, recently described her own encounter with the Sabbath. Coming from a country that is perpetually on the go, with stores open 24 hours a day, the idea of not doing work or engaging in business on a particular day seemed restrictive to her at first. But, as time has gone on, she has come to appreciate the Sabbath more and more. "For one thing," she chuckled, "it makes my workaholic husband take a day off!" Then she added reflectively, "It also gives me time to think about the things that I didn't have time to think about before—to slow down so I can be grateful."

Yes, the Sabbath does give us "time to *think*"—and to *remember*. The seventh-day Sabbath reminds us that the same God who provides our daily needs also created us and the world in which we live (*Exodus 16; 20:8–11)*; that the One who has power to liberate us from that which enslaves us has power to re-create us in His image (*Deuteronomy 5:12–15; Ezekiel 20:12)*; and that the One who rested after making a perfect world will rest once again after He has restored the earth to its original perfection and peace (*Isaiah 66:22–23)*. Though we may take time for God on any day of the week, there is only one day in each week that God Himself blessed and endorsed as a day to put aside all our usual activities and devote to Him. As we honor God on this day, we have a special sense that we are meeting with God *at a time of His choosing* and that the One who originally set the day apart for holy use will *use that holy time to mold us back into His image.*

> ". . . The Sabbath is a gift from God given to humanity right from the beginning. . . . A vacation with God planned from the beginning to be enjoyed into eternity."—Don Postema (pastor of the Campus Chapel at the University of Michigan, Ann Arbor), *Catch Your Breath: God's Invitation to Sabbath Rest*, pp. 5, 15.

So why is it that so many Christians are willing to do without this wonderful Sabbath experience? Let's explore the four basic perspectives of those who excuse themselves and others from observing the seventh-day Sabbath.

2

Four fundamental perspectives on no longer observing the seventh-day Sabbath

1 *"Christians are not under law, but under grace."* Those who hold this first perspective excuse Christians from keeping the seventh-day Sabbath because they assume that not being under the law means not being bound by the Ten Commandments. They reach this sweeping conclusion by linking Paul's statement in *Romans 6:14,* ". . . ye are not under the law, but under grace" with the *assumed* nailing of the law to Jesus' cross in *Colossians 2:14–17* (see **Q8** in back). Some have gone so far as to say that God did away with the commandments because "we could never keep that old law anyway."

Though the discontinuance of the law was once widely taught, in recent years, many Christians have recognized that this "shotgun blast" to the "heart" of the commandments has accomplished too much. It has not only eliminated the unwanted Sabbath commandment, but it has also crippled the effect of the other nine and has left society to stumble along without a clear definition of right and wrong.

The claim that the commandments have been abolished is directly contradicted by statements by John Wesley and Dr. D. James Kennedy:

". . . the moral law, contained in the Ten Commandments, and enforced by the prophets, He did not take away. It was not the design of His coming to revoke any part of this. This is a law which can never be broken . . . Every part of this law must remain in force upon all mankind, and in all ages; as not depending either on time or place, or any other circumstances

7

liable to change, but on the nature of God, and the nature of man, and their unchangeable relation to each other." —**John Wesley** ([1703–1791] Anglican clergyman and founder of Methodism), *Sermons on Several Occasions,* vol. 1, no. 25.

"'... God forbid that we do away with the law through faith. Yea, we establish the law' [Romans 3:31]. As the Old Testament promised, the commandments of God—the law of God—would one day be written upon the fleshly tablets of the heart

[Hebrews 8:10]. And so now they are. And so they become the guide for a Christian, whose great desire, having been saved by grace through faith alone, is now how can he please his Savior." —**D. James Kennedy**, *The Coral Ridge Hour,* September 9, 2001.

The problem for many is that they fail to recognize the continuing value of the Commandments and their role for the Christian (on this point, see **Q9** in back).

Notice **Billy Graham**'s response to the questions: *Do the Ten Commandments have anything to do with Christianity? How important are they?*

"The Ten Commandments give a concise statement of God's moral laws and they have never been set aside. They embody man's responsibility to God and his relationship with his fellowmen. God still demands that He alone shall be worshiped; that we worship Him in spirit and not through idols or images; that we honor

His name and not profane it; that we remember His day and keep it holy or separated from other days; that we honor our parents; that we do not commit murder or adultery; that we do not steal, bear false witness, nor covet things not belonging to us. Jesus Christ summarized the Ten Commandments thus: loving God with all our beings and our neighbors as ourselves. We cannot keep these commandments in our own strength, but only through faith in Jesus Christ, trusting in His help to overcome temptations and to live in a way that is pleasing to Him." —*Billy Graham Answers Your Questions,* p. 45, 46.

The ten precepts of the law define sin and bring conviction to those who break them. They remind us of right and wrong and are a moral safeguard for our relationships with God and our fellow men (*Romans 4:15; 5:13; 7:7; James 1:25*).

". . . Sin is the transgression of the law." 1 John 3:4.

". . . by the law is the knowledge of sin." Romans 3:20.

But what does the phrase "under the law" mean? Is it the same as keeping the commandments? No, indeed. Paul distinguishes between being "under the law" (keeping the whole Jewish ceremonial system, including circumcision) and obeying God's commandments (*1 Corinthians 7:19; Romans 2:25, 26*). Under the New Covenant, we do not need to come "under the law" to be saved, but once we have been saved, *we will willingly keep God's commandments.*

Before God gave Moses the written tablets of the law, men understood that God had a moral standard. (Knowledge of each of the commandments can be documented before Sinai: **1** *Exodus 15:11;* **2** *Genesis 35:2–4;* **3** *Genesis 24:2–3;* **4** *Genesis 2:1; Exodus 16:28;* **5** *Genesis 9:22–27;* **6** *Genesis 4:8–13; 50:17;* **7** *Genesis 39:7–9;* **8** *Genesis 44:8;* **9** *Genesis 4:9; 27:24;* **10** *Genesis 3:6; 14:23; Exodus 18:21*). However, because human beings were prone to rebel against God and violate His standards, God codified the standard of human behavior at Sinai to make their violation more obvious (*Romans 5:20*), adding the symbolic sacrifices and offerings of the *ceremonial* system to instruct them about the "atonement"—the sacrifice of the Lamb that would bring us back into harmony with God (*Galatians 3:19; Romans 3:25; 2 Corinthians 5:19*). Agreeing to this covenant, Israel was put "under the law" in two different senses: they would be under it as their guardian and teacher to bring them to Christ (*Galatians 3:24)* and they would be under its condemnation for having broken its *moral* requirements (*Romans 7:9*).

Under the New Covenant of grace, we are no longer under the tutelage of the *ceremonial* law or the condemnation of the *moral* law. When Christ died on the cross, the veil of the temple was torn in two, signaling that the *symbolism* of the ceremonial law (see **Q8** in back) had been superseded by the *reality* of Christ's New Covenant ministry, which brings us *under* the dominion of God's grace through faith, freeing us from the dominion of sin (*Romans 6:14*).

But neither faith nor grace does away with the *moral* law or obedience to it (*Romans 3:31*). Paul, who declares that we are saved by grace, also calls for obedience to God's commandments (*Ephesians 2:8, 9; 6:1, 2*), and emphasizes that not being "under law" but "under grace" gives us no license to continue sinning (*Romans 6:15),* but, rather, empowers us to live out God's love and fulfill His law (*Romans 13:8*).

2 *"The fourth commandment contains a 'generic Sabbath' command."* Those with this perspective excuse Christians from keeping the seventh-day Sabbath by treating the fourth commandment as a generic command to keep *one day in seven.* In an article entitled, "Is Saturday or Sunday the True Sabbath?" on his *CBN* website, **Pat Robertson**, a major proponent of this view, writes:

"I think the true Sabbath is a day of rest—one out of seven days. Jesus said, 'The Sabbath was made for man, and not man for the Sabbath' (Mark 2:27). By that He meant that God has set up a cyclical type of existence for us, where it is absolutely imperative that we take a break in our work to rest, to be refreshed, to think of things of the Spirit, and to worship Him. Moslems celebrate Friday, Jews Saturday, and Christians Sunday. It is hard to say that one day has any benefit over another."

By recognizing the link between the Sabbath and the seventh day of creation, the *Catholic Catechism* contradicts the idea of a generic Sabbath.

"In speaking of the sabbath Scripture recalls creation: 'For in six days the Lord made heaven and earth, the sea, and all that is in them, and rested the seventh day; therefore the Lord blessed the sabbath day and hallowed it.' . . . God's action is the model for human action . . . Jesus never fails to respect the holiness of this day. He gives this law its authentic and authoritative interpretation, 'The Sabbath was made for man, not man for the Sabbath.' . . . The Sabbath is the day of the Lord of mercies and a day to honor God. 'The Son of Man is Lord even of the Sabbath.'" —*Catechism of the Catholic Church,* 1994 edition, entries 2169, 2172, 2173, pp. 580, 581.

D. L. Moody ([1837–1899] the most famous evangelist of his time and the founder of the *Moody Bible Institute)* also refutes the idea of a generic Sabbath command (as well as the selective abolishment of the fourth commandment of perspective #**4**), as he traces the Sabbath back to its origin in the garden of Eden:

"The Sabbath was binding in Eden, and it has been in force ever since. This fourth commandment begins with the word 'remember,' showing that the Sabbath already existed when God wrote this law on the tables of stone at Sinai. How can men claim that this one commandment has been done away with when they will admit that the other nine are still binding?" —D. L. Moody, *Weighed and Wanting,* p. 47.

Clearly, *the Sabbath is linked specifically to the seventh day because of the seventh day of the creation week (Genesis 2:1–3).* The Sabbath commandment is *not* generic. ". . . the *seventh day* is the Sabbath of the Lord thy God." God doesn't leave it to us to pick out our own particular day.

3 *"The Sabbath's sanctity has been transferred to Sunday."* This third perspective excuses Christians from keeping the seventh-day Sabbath by claiming that, though God did give the Jews the seventh-day Sabbath, He transferred the sanctity of the Sabbath to Sunday, making it the day for Christian worship. There are two suggested conduits of such a change. Either the transfer of sanctity came through Jesus or the Apostles or it came through authority granted the Church to make such a change.

Because much of the Church eventually adopted Sunday observance, many Church authorities have assumed that either Jesus or the Apostles made the change, as we see in the following quotations:

"I am confused as to which day to worship God. Some of my friends say it is Saturday, and some say that it is Sunday. Would you please give me Scriptures as to which day is the day on which to worship?

"The concept that we are to be religious just one day a week is not in accordance with the teaching of Christ. In Acts we read of the Spirit-filled Christians: 'And they continued steadfastly (continuously) in the apostles' doctrine and fellowship, and in breaking of bread and in prayers . . . and the Lord added to the church daily such as should be saved.'

"The Sabbath, as taught in the Old Testament, was the seventh day of the week; but the Bible shows that from the time of the resurrection onward, Christians worshiped on the first day of the week." —Billy Graham, "The better life," *Billy Graham Answers Your Questions,* p. 51.

"Jesus, after his resurrection, changed the Sabbath from the seventh to the first day of the week . . . When Jesus gave instructions for this change we are not told, but very likely during the time when he spake to his apostles of the things pertaining to his kingdom. Acts i, 3. This is probably one of the many unrecorded things which Jesus did. John xx, 30; xxi, 25." —Amos Binney, *Theological Compend,* 1875, p. 171.

"The day is now changed from the seventh to the first day, . . . but as we meet with no Scriptural direction for the change, we may conclude it was done by the authority of the church, under the guidance of the apostles." —*Explanation of the Church Catechism (Protestant Episcopal),* p. 8.

The truth is, there are no Scriptures which tell us that "from the time of the resurrection onward, Christians worshiped on the first day of the week." Not even the verses most often cited in favor of Sunday observance establish such a claim (see **Q5** in back). Likewise, there are no Scriptures which indicate that Jesus or any of the Apostles ever called for a change in the Christian day of worship—either in their teachings or by their example.

"There was never any formal or authoritative change from the Jewish Seventh Day Sabbath to the Christian First Day observance." —William O. Carver *(Baptist), Sabbath Observance,* p. 49.

In light of such evidence, Catholic and *some* Protestant authorities explain that the transfer was made by God-granted Church authority.

"Q. Which is the Sabbath day?

"A. Saturday is the Sabbath day.

"Q. Why do we observe Sunday instead of Saturday?

"A. We observe Sunday instead of Saturday because the Catholic Church transferred the solemnity from Saturday to Sunday." —Peter Geiermann, CSSR (Catholic priest of Mt. St. Clement's College, De Soto, Missouri, whose catechism received the "apostolic blessing" of Pope Pius X, Jan. 25, 1910), *The Convert's Catechism of Catholic Doctrine,* 1957 edition, p. 50.

"We have made the change from the seventh day to the first day, from Saturday to Sunday, on the authority of the one holy, catholic, apostolic church of Christ." —Bishop Seymour *(Episcopalian), Why We Keep Sunday.*

The thought that the leaders of God's Church believed that God gave them the authority to alter one of His Ten Commandments, substituting a human pronouncement for one of His own commandments and calling it true worship seems almost incredible. Of those who would make such a substitution, Jesus said:

"But in vain they do worship me, teaching for doctrines the commandments of men." Matthew 15:9.

Perhaps, the Church honestly believed it was correct in putting *human tradition* before *God's Word.* But, in this, they did not follow the counsel of the Apostle Peter to the religious authorities of his day:

"We ought to obey God rather than men." Acts 5:29.

4 *"Christians are to keep a 'spiritual' Sabbath."* Under this perspective, there are no literal sabbaths for Christians to keep—the seventh-day Sabbath is classified as a non-binding ceremonial observance (and Sunday is not a day of rest). When first articulated, this view rejected the seventh-day Sabbath on the basis of the spiritualized Old Testament and allegorical "eighth day" interpretations of the early Catholic Fathers. (See under Pseudo-Barnabas.)

"'Your new moons and your sabbaths I cannot endure' (Isaiah 1:13). You perceive how He speaks: Your present sabbaths are not acceptable to me but that which I had made in giving rest to all things, I shall make a beginning of the eighth day, that is a beginning of another world. Wherefore also, we keep the *eighth day* with joyfulness, a day also in which Jesus rose from the dead." —*Epistle of Barnabas,* ch. 16 (*c.* 135 A. D), *emphasis supplied.*

"'Now, sirs,' I said, 'it is possible for us to show how the *eighth day* possessed a certain mysterious import, which the seventh day did not possess, and which was promulgated by God through these rites [i.e., circumcision on the eighth day].'" —Justin Martyr, *Dialogue with Trypho,* ch. 24 (*c.* 150 A.D), *emphasis supplied.*

Admittedly, few today use the eighth day argument as a reason for no longer observing the seventh-day Sabbath. Yet many still consider the *literal* Sabbath of the fourth commandment irrelevant for Christians since, they say, "Christ gives *spiritual* rest every day of the week." Others, who do not wish to so casually dismiss a divine commandment, take great pains to "protect" the spiritual essence of the Sabbath and the law by distinguishing between the *precept* of the Sabbath (which they see as *moral)* and the *fixed time* for the Sabbath (which they see as *ceremonial),* agreeing to only remove that portion of the ten which they believe threatens the commandments' spiritual vitality.

A number of evangelical teachers, such as *Urban Alternative* speaker, **Dr. Tony Evans,** espouse such a "spiritual" view. In a recent, mid-day radio call-in program, Dr. Evans stated that, even though the fourth commandment calls for worship on Saturday, Sunday is the new day for worship because the Sabbath was "ceremonial" and because the fourth commandment is the only commandment of the ten that is not restated in the New Testament (on this point, see **Q2** in back).

Though the thought that Christ freed us from keeping literal sabbaths by giving us "sabbath rest" every day may sound very "spiritual," on closer examination, we realize that this teaching overlooks two important facts: Jesus taught that the Sabbath was established for man's practical benefit (*Mark 2:27, 28*) and Isaiah declared that the Sabbath can be kept in a spiritual manner (*Isaiah 58:13, 14*)—a fact with which the early church would have agreed (see Bishop Taylor, *"they kept the Sabbath . . . after the spiritual manner"*). The literal keeping of the Sabbath is just as valuable in reminding us of the spiritual truth behind it as participation in actual baptism or in the Lord's supper are in reminding us of the spiritual truths behind them.

Although they probably wouldn't think of it in this way, by their dismissal of the seventh-day Sabbath as being *ceremonial* in nature, proponents of this view are actually casting the Commandment Giver in a negative light for His "oversight" in including a *ceremonial* element in His great *moral* set of ten (an "oversight," incidentally, which was only caught and corrected after the death of the last Apostle by a Church that was drifting away from its early faith and simplicity). And, shocking as it may seem, their attempts to protect the "essence" of the Ten Commandments from wholesale "abortion," by removal of a part or the whole of the Sabbath command, amount to nothing less than the "selective reduction" of a holy commandment of God!

When it comes to this perspective, what position does the Catholic Church take? The 1994 *Catholic Catechism* contains some curious statements which appear, at first, to support the "spiritual" view, but actually argue in favor of a transfer of "ceremonial observance."

"Jesus rose from the dead 'on the first day of the week.' Because it is the 'first day,' the day of Christ's Resurrection recalls the first creation. Because it is the 'eighth day' following the sabbath, it symbolizes the new creation ushered in by Christ's Resurrection.

"Sunday is expressly distinguished from the sabbath which it follows chronologically every week; for Christians its *ceremonial observance* replaces that of the sabbath." —*Catechism of the Catholic Church,* 1994 edition, entries 2174 and 2175 , p. 581, *emphasis supplied.*

Discounting the fact that it was *the seventh day* that God established to call our minds back to the first creation and *not the first day*, we ask, what sense would it have made for God to have done away with the observance of one day because of its supposed *ceremonial* nature only to have the Church replace it with another day for "*ceremonial* observance"? (And what would make observing Sunday any more *spiritual* than observing the day God asked us to observe?) The seventh-day Sabbath was *not* a *ceremonial* oversight on God's part. Rather, *it was a thoughtful gift from a loving God, given on the seventh day of the creation week to be enjoyed by mankind each successive seventh day thereafter. And do we not need such a gift all the more in these frantically busy times of ours?*

3

Christians still need "Sabbath rest."

*I*n his newspaper column, "MY ANSWER," Dr. Billy Graham, blending the four perspectives, acknowledges the Christian's need for special times of worship.

"Dear DR. GRAHAM: Why do some Christians hold Saturday as their day of worship instead of Sunday? —F.R.

"DEAR F.R.: Saturday is the seventh day of the week and, as such, was (and is) the Jewish day of worship in accordance with the Old Testament. The command to set aside one day out of seven, for worship and rest from normal labor is found in the Ten Commandments: 'Remember the Sabbath day to keep it holy . . . the seventh day is the Sabbath of the Lord thy God . . . for in six days the Lord made heaven and earth, the sea, and all that in them is, and rested the seventh day: wherefore the Lord blessed the sabbath day, and hallowed it' (Exo. 20:8, 10, 11).

"The early Christians realized that they were not saved by keeping the Old Testament law, but by God's grace. Early Christians who had been Jews probably kept Saturday as their day of worship, but as time went on Sunday replaced Saturday, largely because Jesus had been raised from the dead on a Sunday.

"While there are some Christians who still hold Saturday instead of Sunday as their day of worship, this should not be an issue that divides honest believers. Paul only mentions the Sabbath once directly. He says, 'Let no man therefore judge you . . . in respect of an holy day . . . or of the Sabbath days' (Colossians 2:16). The important thing is that we serve God every day of our lives and especially set apart times of worship. When we truly love God above all else, we will want to 'enter into his gates with thanksgiving, and into his courts with praise' (Psalm 100:4)."

Dr. Graham is right about one thing: those who love God *should* meet with Him in His special "set apart" time for worship, and even more because of the intensity of life in our modern times, as D.L. Moody and Pat Robertson have pointed out:

"I honestly believe that this commandment is just as binding to-day as it ever was. I have talked with men who have said that it has been abrogated, but they have never been able to point to any place in the Bible where God repealed it. When Christ was on earth, He did nothing to set it aside; He freed it from the traces under which the scribes and Pharisees had put it, and gave it its true place. 'The Sabbath was made for man, not man for the Sabbath.' It is just as practicable and as necessary for men to-day as it ever was—in fact, more than ever, because we live in such an intense age." —Dwight L. Moody, *Weighed and Wanting,* pp. 46, 47.

"God understands human nature and he knows more than we will ever know what we need to keep those first three commandments—and that is a day set aside every week to honor him. . . . It's absolutely essential that a society, that a people, that individuals have a periodic day of rest, that they have a periodic day of worship, that they have a periodic day when they can focus their attention on God Almighty and take it off of commerce. And that is why it is so devastating, in our society, to see city after city opening full-blast on Sunday. . . .

". . . As people lose sight of their walk with God, they also will lose sight of their obligations to one another and they will substitute, for God's laws, man's concepts of what is right and what is wrong. . . .

"Now, there are some people who say, . . . the real Sabbath is on Saturday. Well, you're right. The Sabbath is indeed Friday night sundown to Saturday sundown. . . ." —Pat Robertson, "A Day Made for You."

We applaud these men for encouraging Christians to give God a special day each week. However, we cannot help but puzzle over the inference that a person can commemorate the *seventh-day* memorial of creation, dictated in a "binding" commandment of God, by worshipping on the *first day* of the week (and especially when one acknowledges, as Pat Robertson does, that the Sabbath is really on Saturday).

4

Most Christian scholars admit there is no scriptural "Sunday Sabbath."

*C*hristian Sabbath not in the Scriptures. ". . . the Christian Sabbath is not in the Scriptures, and was not by the primitive church, called *the sabbath* . . ." —Timothy Dwight ([1752–1817] *Congregationalist* president of Yale University from 1795–1817), *Theology,* sermon 107, 1818 ed., vol. IV, p. 41.

Sunday observance is not Sabbath keeping. ". . . it is quite clear that however rigidly or devotedly we may spend Sunday, we are not keeping the Sabbath . . . The Sabbath was founded on a specific Divine command. We can plead no such command for the obligation to observe Sunday . . . There is not a single sentence in the New Testament to suggest that we incur any penalty by violating the supposed sanctity of Sunday." —Dr. R. W. Dale (*Congregationalist*), *The Ten Commandments,* pp. 100–101.

Sunday was a regular work day. "Until well into the second century [a hundred years after Christ] we do not find the slightest indication in our sources that Christians marked Sunday by any kind of abstention from work." —W. Rordorf, *Sunday,* p. 157.

Sunday never called Sabbath in the Scriptures. "The first day of the week is commonly called the Sabbath. This is a mistake. The Sabbath of the Bible was the day just preceding the first day of the week. The first day of the week is never called the Sabbath anywhere in the entire Scriptures. It is also an error to talk about the change of the Sabbath from Saturday to Sunday. There is not in any place in the Bible any intimation of such a change."—*First-Day Observance* (*Christian*), pp. 17, 19.

No Scripture to sustain Sunday observance. "There is no word, no hint in the New Testament about abstaining from work on Sunday. The observance of Ash Wednesday, or Lent, stands exactly on the same footing as the observance of Sunday. Into the rest of Sunday no Divine Law enters."—Canon Eyton *(Presbyterian), The Ten Commandments.*

"And where are we told in the Scriptures that we are to keep the first day at all? We are commanded to keep the seventh; but we are nowhere commanded to keep the first day. The reason why we keep the first day of the week holy instead of the seventh is for the same reason that we observe many other things,—not because the Bible, but because the church, has enjoined it."—Isaac Williams (1802–1865, *Anglican), Plain Sermons On The Catechism,* vol. 1, pp. 334, 336.

"It must be confessed that there is no law in the New Testament concerning the first day."—McClintock and Strong, *Cyclopedia of Biblical Theological and Ecclesiastical Literature,* vol. 9, p. 196.

"There is nothing in Scripture that requires us to keep Sunday rather than Saturday as a holy day."—Dr. Harold Lindsell (former editor of *Christianity Today), Christianity Today,* November 5, 1976.

"But they err in teaching that Sunday has taken the place of the Old Testament Sabbath and therefore must be kept as the seventh day had to be kept by the children of Israel. . . . These churches err in their teaching, for scripture has in no way ordained the first day of the week in place of the Sabbath. There is simply no law in the New Testament to that effect."—John Theodore Mueller (*Lutheran), Sabbath or Sunday,* pp. 15, 16.

The change did not come from the Apostles. "The sacred name of the seventh day is Sabbath. That fact is too clear to require argument. The truth is stated in concise terms: 'The seventh day is the Sabbath of the Lord thy God.' . . . On this point the plain teaching of the Word has been admitted in all ages. Except to certain special sabbaths appointed in Levitical law, and these invariably governed by the month rather than the week, the Bible in all its utterances never, no, not once, applies the name Sabbath to any other day. . . . Not once did they [the disciples] apply the Sabbath law to the first day of the

21

week,—that folly was left for a later age, nor did they pretend that the first day supplanted the seventh." —Joseph Judson Taylor (*Southern Baptist*), *The Sabbatic Question, 1914,* pp. 16, 41.

"Take which you will, either the 'fathers' or the moderns, and we shall find no Lord's Day instituted by any apostolic mandate, no sabbath set on foot by them upon the first day of the week." —Dr. Peter Heylyn (*Church of England*), quoted in *History of the Sabbath,* Part 2, chapter 1, p. 410.

"The festival of Sunday, like all other festivals, was always only a human ordinance, and it was far from the intentions of the apostles to establish a Divine command in this respect, far from them, and from the early apostolic Church, to transfer the laws of the Sabbath to Sunday. . . ." —Augustus Neander (*Lutheran*), *The History of the Christian Religion and Church,* Rose's translation, 1843, p. 186.

The change did not originate during the apostolic age or as a result of apostolic authority. "We must conclude that it is barely imaginable that first-day Sabbath observance commenced before the Jerusalem council. Nor can we stop there; we must go on to maintain that first-day Sabbath observance cannot easily be understood as a phenomenon of the apostolic age or of apostolic authority at all." —D. A. Carson, *From Sabbath to Lord's Day,* 1982, pp. 135–136.

Record of change comes branded with the mark of paganism. "There was and is a command to keep holy the Sabbath day, but that Sabbath day was not Sunday. It will however be readily said, and with some show of triumph, that the Sabbath was transferred from the seventh to the first day of the week, with all its duties, privileges and sanctions. Earnestly desiring information on this subject, which I have studied for many years, I ask, where can the record of such a transaction be found? Not in the New Testament—absolutely not. There is no scriptural evidence of the change of the Sabbath institution from the seventh to the first day of the week.

"I wish to say that this Sabbath question, in this aspect of it, is the gravest and *most perplexing question* connected with Christian institutions which at present claims attention from Christian people; and the only reason that it is not a more disturbing element in Christian thought and in religious discussion is because the Christian world has settled down content on the conviction that somehow a transference has taken place at the beginning of Christian history.

"To me it seems unaccountable that Jesus, during three years' intercourse with His disciples, often conversing with them upon the Sabbath question, discussing it in some of its various aspects, freeing it from its false glosses [of Jewish traditions], never alluded to any transference of the day; also, that during the forty days of His resurrection life, no such thing was intimated. Nor, so far as we know, did the Spirit, which was given to bring to their remembrance all things whatsoever that He had said unto them, deal with this question. Nor yet did the inspired apostles, in preaching the gospel, founding churches, counseling and instructing those founded, discuss or approach the subject.

"Of course, I quite well know that Sunday did come into use in early Christian history as a religious day, as we learn from the Christian Fathers and other sources. But what a pity that it comes *branded with the mark of Paganism,* and christened with the name of the sun-god, then adopted and sanctified by the Papal apostasy, and bequeathed as a sacred legacy to Protestantism." —Dr. E. T. Hiscox (author of *The Baptist Manual), New York Examiner,* November 13, 1893, *emphasis supplied.*

Who has the right to change Sabbath to Sunday? "For, when there could not be produced one solitary place in the Holy Scriptures which testified that either the Lord Himself or the apostles had ordered such a transfer of the Sabbath to Sunday, then it was not easy to answer the question: Who has transferred the Sabbath, and who has had the right to do it?" —George Sverdrup (*Lutheran Free Church*), "A New Day," *Sunday and Its Observance,* p. 342.

There can be no change without a new creation to be commemorated. "If it [the Sabbath] yet exist, let us observe it according to law. And if it does not exist [Campbell believed that it did not], let us abandon a mock observance of another day for it. 'But,' say some, 'it was *changed* from the seventh to the first day.' Where? When? And by whom? No man can tell. No, it never was changed, nor could it be, unless creation was to be gone through again: for the reason assigned must be changed before the observance or respect to the reason, can

be changed!! It is all old wives' fables to talk of the 'change of the Sabbath' from the seventh to the first day. If it be changed, it was that August personage changed it who changes times and laws *ex officio*—I think his name is DOCTOR ANTICHRIST. . . ."—**Alexander Campbell**, *The Christian Baptist,* February 2, 1824, vol. 1, no. 7.

In *Daniel 7:25* we find the "personage" to whom Campbell refers, a personage that claims to have had the authority to change God's law (a subject which is further explored in the section, ***Protestants, Catholics, and the Authority for Sunday Worship***).

"And he shall speak great words against the most High, and shall wear out the saints of the most High, <u>and think to change times and laws</u>: and they shall be given into his hand until a time and times and the dividing of time." Daniel 7:25.

Some Christian authorities deny that the change from Sabbath to Sunday involved any kind of an innovation on the part of the Church, pointing to the writings of the early Church Fathers as evidence that the exaltation of the Sunday "Lord's Day" was a natural progression of Apostolic thinking.

What is the truth? Do the Church Fathers represent a further development of the writings of the Apostles, or are they something else? Let's examine the evidence and see.

5

Are the Church Fathers the "missing link" of Sunday succession?

*R*esonating the sentiment of many evangelical writers, Walter Martin, in his book, *The Kingdom of the Cults,* confidently asserts:

"The Church Fathers provide a mass of evidence that the first day of the week, not the seventh, is the Lord's Day. Some of this evidence is here submitted for the reader's consideration. In company with the overwhelming majority of historians and scholars, we believe that not only the New Testament but the following citations refute Sabbatarianism. We have yet to see any systematic answer to what the Christian Church always believed." —Walter Martin, *The Kingdom of the Cults,* p. 460.

Is Mr. Martin's assertion correct? Has the Christian Church *always* believed that Sunday is the Lord's Day, as his carefully-worded statement implies? Do the "Church Fathers provide a mass of evidence" that Sunday and not Saturday is the "Lord's Day"? Should the use, in time, of the term "Lord's day" by the *Fathers* be heralded as the "missing link" of Sunday succession, as evidence that Christian leaders have always believed that they should observe Sunday rather than the Sabbath?

If the truth be told, there is neither evidence in the New Testament or in the *Fathers* that the Apostles advocated the substitution of the first day "Lord's Day" for the seventh-day "Sabbath of the Lord thy God."

"Not any ecclesiastical writer of the first three centuries attributed the origin of Sunday observance either to Christ or to His apostles."—Sir William Domville (*Church of England*), *Examination of the Six Texts*, pp. 6, 7 (supplement).

In the following pages, we will examine the testimony of the *Fathers* (using Mr. Martin's order), giving special attention to the internal and external issues which disqualify them as spokesmen for "what the Church has always believed" about the day for worship.

1. IGNATIUS, BISHOP OF ANTIOCH (115 A.D.):

"If, then, those who walk in the ancient practices attain to newness of hope, no longer observing the Sabbath, but fashioning their lives after the Lord's Day on which our life also arose through Him, that we may be found disciples of Jesus Christ, our only teacher."

FOCAL ISSUE: The mistaken reading, "Lord's *Day*," makes the Old Testament prophets appear to have abandoned the Sabbath in favor of Sunday.

"About A.D. 115 Ignatius, Bishop of Antioch, traveled through the Roman province of Asia on his way to martyrdom in Rome. On this journey he penned letters to various of the Asian churches, giving them counsel in view of Judaizing and Gnostic tendencies that appeared to be creeping in. Ignatius' so-called 'Lord's day' statement occurs in chapter 9 of his letter to the Magnesians, and reads as follows from a commonly accepted edition of the Greek text: *mēketi sabbatizontes alla kata kuriakēn zōntes*—'No longer sabbatizing, but living according to the Lord's.' It should be noted that the Greek word for 'day' (*hēmeran*, in the accusative case) is *not* in the text.

"The manuscript evidence favors, however, a longer version of the Greek—a version that contains the word *zōēn*, 'life.' This word has been omitted by modern editors in the commonly accepted Greek wording given above. The actual text, as found in the earliest existing manuscript, reads as follows: *mēketi sabbatizontes alla kata kuriakēn zōēn zōntes*. The normal rendering of this expression (unless a cognate accusative was intended) would be: 'no longer sabbatizing, but living according to the Lord's life.'

"Probably the strongest evidence that not *days* but *ways of life* are in view in this passage comes from a consideration of the entire context. The persons to whom Ignatius refers as 'no longer sabbatizing, but living according to the Lord's' are the *Old Testament prophets*. In chapter 8:1, 2 he had declared that 'if we are still living according to Judaism we admit that we have not received grace; for the most divine prophets lived in accord with Jesus Christ.' In chapter 9:1, 2 he goes on to declare, 'If, therefore, those who lived in ancient ways came to new hope, no longer sabbatizing, but living according to the Lord's [life], in which also our life arose through him and his death, . . . how shall we be able to live without him of whom even the prophets were disciples in the Spirit—looking forward to him as their teacher?'

"It is also worth noting that the fourth-century interpolator of Ignatius did not see in this passage a conflict between two different days, for he approved the observance of *both* days. In his version of this passage in Magnesians 9 . . . he prescribes that the Sabbath should be kept in a 'spiritual manner,' after which the 'Lord's day' should also be observed.

"A distinguished patristic scholar, Robert A. Kraft, has provided the following translation of the original Ignatius of the early second century: If, then, those who walked in the ancient customs [i.e., the aforementioned prophets] came to have a new hope, no longer 'sabbatizing' but living in accord with the Lord's life—in which life there sprang up also our life through him and through his death." —Kenneth A. Strand, *The Sabbath in Scripture and History*, pp. 348, 349, *bracketed material in the original.*

If Ignatius had literally meant that the ancient prophets had ceased to keep the Sabbath, then he would have certainly disqualified himself as an expositor of the Old Testament, for the prophets did indeed observe the Sabbath (as did Jesus and Paul)! "Of course, they kept the Sabbath," someone will say, "they were *born* under the law, but we Christians are under grace." That is true, but keeping the Sabbath is no more legalistic than honoring our parents. Besides, there is not a single indication that Jesus ever intended for His followers to discard the Sabbath. If He were only going to have them toss it in the "recycle bin," why did He expend so much effort to remove the tarnish of human tradition that had obscured its underlying spiritual luster and practical intent? And, if Paul saw a conflict between the gospel and the Sabbath, would he not have ceased to keep it? But he *did* keep it, not for the purpose of justifying himself with God (*Romans 3:20*), but out of a desire to assemble with other believers who were participating in the blessed Sabbath rest left to the people of God (*Hebrews 4:9; 10:25*) in God's *holy* commandment in His *holy* law (*Romans 7:12*). When seen from a spiritual perspective, the Sabbath commandment actually combats salvation by works, for the Sabbath is not about what one does, but about resting in what God has already done (*Hebrews 4:9–11*). We enter into the rest that God initiated in Eden and confirmed at Calvary. With Jesus' dying words, "Into thy hands I commend my spirit" (*Luke 23:46*), He affirmed His trust in His Father and then rested the Sabbath in His Father's love.

Thus, properly understood, "living life according to the Lord's life" means, living by the same Spirit that empowered His life and walking "as He walked" (*1 John 2:6*), we will follow His example in every area of our lives, including resting and worshipping in spirit and in truth (*John 4:23*) on the Sabbath. But, as we shall see from the *Fathers*, following Christ's example was not always the prime motivation for the Church that claimed to be the guardians of His truth.

2. JUSTIN MARTYR (100–165):

"And on the day called Sunday, all who live in cities or in the country gather together in one place and memoirs of the apostles or the writings of the prophets are read, as long as time permits. . . . Sunday is the day on which we all hold our common assembly because it is the first day on which God, having wrought a change in the darkness in matter, made the world: and Jesus Christ our Saviour on the same day rose from the dead."

FOCAL ISSUES: (1) **non-biblical reasoning which ties the light of the sun with Jesus' resurrection and (2) the influence of pagan philosophy.**

Say that again, Justin, why is it that Christians worship on Sunday?

"Justin Martyr (*c.* A.D. 100–165) emphasizes that Christians assemble 'on the day called Sunday . . . because it is the first day on which God, having wrought a change in the darkness and matter, made the world.' Is the nexus [*link*] between the day of the Sun and the creation of light on the first day a pure coincidence? It hardly seems so, not only because Justin himself in his *Dialogue with Trypho* explicitly compares the devotion that pagans render to the Sun with that which Christians offer to Christ, who is 'more blazing and bright than the rays of the sun,' but also because the coincidence between the creation of light on the first day and the veneration of the Sun on the selfsame day is clearly established by several Fathers. . . . Eusebius (*c.* A.D. 260–340), for instance, refers explicitly to the motifs of the light and of the day of the Sun to justify Sunday worship: '*In this day of light,* first day and *true day of the sun,* when we gather after the interval of six days, we celebrate the holy and spiritual Sabbaths. . . . In fact, it is on this day of the creation of the world that God said: "*Let there be light;* and there was light.*" It is also on this day that the Sun of Justice has risen for our souls.'" —Bacchiocchi, *The Sabbath in Scripture and History,* p. 141.

Justin's logic for keeping Sunday seems therefore to be based *not* upon a command of the Lord or of Paul, but upon an association of the creation of light, the day of the sun, and the day of the resurrection. (Curiously enough, the sun was made on the *fourth* day and is only linked to the *first* day by pagan sun worship.) How did Justin come to make such an association?

What was Justin's background?

Before learning of Christ, Justin had been an avid student of philosophy. After his conversion, he continued to wear his philosopher's gown as a token that he had attained "the only true philosophy."

"Of course, like the other apologists of the second century, Justin was, in his theology, to a great extent influenced by, and dependent upon, Greek philosophy (cf. Photius, *Bibliotheca,* cod. 125: 'He is a man who has climbed the heights of philosophy, Greek as well as foreign; he is overflowing with much learning and the riches of knowledge.') Early Christian writers referred to him as 'St. Justin Martyr and Philosopher' (cf. Anastasius) or '*St. Justin Philosopher and Martyr'* (cf. John of Damascus)." —foreword, *The Fathers of the Church: Writings of Saint Justin Martyr*, p. 17, *emphasis supplied.*

Because of his background and the way he was introduced to Christianity, Justin could see no value in the Sabbath for Christians. In chapter 23 of *Dialogue with Trypho,* Justin describes the "certain old man," who had introduced Justin to Christianity as the fulfillment of true philosophy, dissuading him from keeping the Sabbath with the words: "Remain as you were born." In chapter 24 of *Dialogue with Trypho*, Justin exalts the "eighth day" (Sunday) over the seventh.

". . . With the Jews, contended in particular Justin Martyr, in his dialogue with Trypho; and likewise Tertullian; but neither of them, in the best manner; because they were not acquainted with the language and history of the Hebrews, and did not duly consider the subject." —Mosheim, *Ecclesiastical History,* book 1, cent. 2, part 2, chap. 3, sec. 7.

One glaring example of this is Justin's mistaken assertion that the Sabbath was given to the Jews "as a distinguishing mark, to set them off from other nations and from us Christians" so that the Jews only "might suffer affliction" (Justin, *Dialogue,* chaps. 16 and 21). A quick look at the Old Testament prophets reveals quite the contrary. God didn't give the Sabbath for affliction, but for blessing!

"Moreover also I gave them my sabbaths, to be a sign between me and them, that they might know that I am the LORD that sanctify them." Ezekiel 20:12.

"If thou turn away thy foot from the sabbath, from doing thy pleasure on my holy day; and call the sabbath a delight, the holy of the LORD, honourable; and shalt honour him, not doing thine own ways, nor finding thine own pleasure, nor speaking

thine own words: [14] *Then shalt thou delight thyself in the LORD; and I will cause thee to ride upon the high places of the earth, and feed thee with the heritage of Jacob thy father: for the mouth of the LORD hath spoken it." Isaiah 58:13, 14.*

"Blessed is the man that doeth this, and the son of man that layeth hold on it; that keepeth the sabbath from polluting it, and keepeth his hand from doing any evil. [6] *Also the sons of the stranger, that join themselves to the LORD, to serve him, and to love the name of the LORD, to be his servants, every one that keepeth the sabbath from polluting it, and taketh hold of my covenant;* [7] *Even them will I bring to my holy mountain, and make them joyful in my house of prayer: their burnt offerings and their sacrifices shall be accepted upon mine altar; for mine house shall be called an house of prayer for all people." Isaiah 56:2, 6, 7.*

3. THE EPISTLE OF BARNABAS (*c.* 120–150):

"Your new moons and your sabbaths I cannot endure" (Isaiah 1:13). You perceive how He speaks: Your present sabbaths are not acceptable to me but that which I had made in giving rest to all things, I shall make a beginning of the eighth day, that is a beginning of another world. Wherefore also, we keep the *eighth day* with joyfulness, a day also in which Jesus rose from the dead."

FOCAL ISSUES: (1) Reliability of the epistle, (2) influence of Alexandria, and (3) non-biblical reasoning regarding the "eighth day."

How reliable is this epistle?

"As to what is suggested by some, of its having been written by that Barnabas who was the friend and companion of St. Paul, the futility of such a notion is easily to be made apparent from the letter itself; several of the opinions and interpretations of Scripture which it contains having in them so little either of truth, dignity, or force as to render it impossible that they could ever have proceeded from the pen of a man divinely instructed." —Mosheim, *Historical Commentaries,* Century 1, Sec. 53.

"Among the rejected writings must be reckoned also the Acts of Paul, and the so-called Shepherd, and the Apocalypse of Peter, and in addition to these the extant *Epistle of Barnabas,* and the so-called Teachings of the Apostles." —Eusebius, *Church History,* book III, chap. 25, sec. 4. *The Nicene and Post-Nicene Fathers,* vol. I, p. 156, *emphasis supplied.*

The exaltation of Sunday is a "Tale of Two Cities."

"The earliest direct evidence for Christian weekly worship on Sunday comes from second-century Alexandria and Rome. About A.D. 130 Barnabas of Alexandria, in a highly allegorical discourse, declares, 'Wherefore, also, we keep the eighth day [i.e., Sunday] with joyfulness.' Some two decades later Justin Martyr in Rome actually describes in some detail the type of Christian meeting held on Sundays there, possibly as a very early morning service.

"The situation in Rome and Alexandria, however, was not typical of the rest of early Christianity. In these two cities there was an evident early attempt by Christians to terminate observance of the seventh-day

Library of Alexandria

Sabbath, but elsewhere throughout the Christian world Sunday observance simply arose *alongside* observance of Saturday. Two fifth-century church historians, Socrates Scholasticus and Sozomen, describe the situation in the following way: 'For although almost all churches throughout the world celebrate the sacred mysteries [the Lord's supper] on the Sabbath [Saturday] of every week, yet the Christians of Alexandria and at Rome, on account of some ancient tradition, have ceased to do this. The Egyptians in the neighborhood of Alexandria, and the inhabitants of Thebais, hold their religious assemblies on the Sabbath . . . The people of Constantinople, and almost everywhere, assemble together on the Sabbath, as well as on the first day of the

Papal Palace of Rome

week, which custom is never observed at Rome or at Alexandria. . . .'
Thus, even *as late as the fifth century* almost the entire Christian world
observed *both Saturday and Sunday* for special religious services.
Obviously, therefore, Sunday was not considered a substitute for the
Sabbath." —Strand, *The Sabbath in Scripture and History,* pp. 323, 324.

Did Barnabas say that Jesus rose on the "eighth day"?

"Another valuable arsenal of
apologetic techniques to defend
the superiority of Sunday over the
Sabbath was provided by the
symbology of the eighth day. As a
designation for Sunday, this term
first appears in anti-Judaic polemical writings, such as the *Epistle of
Barnabas* and the *Dialogue with Trypho.* It was widely employed in
Christian literature of the first five centuries.

"Such a designation apparently derives from chiliastic-eschato-
logical speculations on the seven-day Creation week (sometimes
called 'cosmic week') prevailing in Jewish and Jewish Christian
circles. The duration of the world was subdivided into seven periods
(or millennia), of which the seventh (identified with the Sabbath)
generally represented paradise restored. At the end of the seventh
period the eternal new eon would dawn, which eon came to be known
as 'the eighth day' since it was the successor to the seventh.

"In the polemic with Sabbath-keepers, the symbology of the
eighth day was applied to Sunday to prove the superiority of the latter
over the Sabbath. A wide range of arguments were drawn not only
from apocalyptic literature but also from the Scriptures, philosophy,
and the natural world. As the eighth eschatological day, Sunday was
defended as the symbol of the new world, superior to the Sabbath,
which represented only the seventh terrestrial millennium. Also, as
the Gnostic ogdoad, Sunday was presented as a symbol of the rest of
spiritual beings in the supercelestial eternal world, found above the
sevenness of this transitory world. Moreover, Sunday could be
prestigiously traced back to the 'prophecies' of the Old Testament,
by means of the Biblical number eight, which the Fathers found in
several references from the Old Testament, such as the eighth day for
circumcision; the eight souls saved from the Flood; the fifteen cubits
(seven plus eight) of the Flood waters above the mountains; the

superscription of Psalms 6 and 11 ('for the eighth day'); the fifteen (seven plus eight) gradual psalms; the saying 'give a portion to seven, or even to eight,' of Ecclesiastes 11:2; the eighth day when Job offered sacrifices; and others. Invested with such 'prophetic' authority, the eighth day could 'legitimately' represent the fulfillment of the reign of the law, allegedly typified by the Sabbath, and the inauguration of the kingdom of grace supposedly exemplified by Sunday. Jerome expressed this view by saying that 'the number seven having been fulfilled, we now rise to the Gospel through the eighth.'

"The polemic use of the symbolism of the eighth day that developed out of apocalyptic, Gnostic, and Biblical sources to prove the superiority of Sunday over the Sabbath corroborates again that Sunday worship arose as a controversial innovation and not as an undisputed apostolic institution. Indeed, when the Sabbath-Sunday controversy subsided, the very name 'eighth day' and its inherent eschatological meaning (used first by Barnabas and afterward by numerous Fathers) was formally and explicitly repudiated as a designation and motivation for Sundaykeeping! John Chrysostom (c. A.D. 347–407), Bishop of Constantinople, provides a most explicit confirmation of this development. After explaining that the eighth day represents exclusively the future life, he affirms categorically: 'It is for this reason that no one calls the Lord's day the eighth day but only first day.'" —Samuele Bacchiocchi, *The Sabbath in Scripture and History,* pp. 143, 144.

It was the hybridized nature of Christianity during this period that helped Sunday to rise so quickly in importance.

"Cross-fertilization of gnostic and catholic theology continued throughout the bitter struggles of the second century . . ." —Carson, *From Sabbath to Lord's Day,* p. 255.

4. IRENAEUS (c. 178):

"The mystery of the Lord's resurrection may not be celebrated on any other day than the Lord's Day."

FOCAL ISSUE: The "Lord's Day" of Irenaeus does not refer to a weekly day of worship, but to an annual Easter celebration.

"A slightly earlier 'Lord's day' reference [than that of *Clement of Alexandria,* see below] (about A.D. 180 or 185) was made by Bishop Irenaeus of Gaul, but Irenaeus appears to have been speaking of Easter Sunday rather than a weekly Sunday: 'This [custom], of not bending the knee upon Sunday, is a symbol of the resurrection, through which we have been set free, by the grace of Christ, from sins, and from death, which has been put to death under Him. Now this custom took its rise from apostolic times, as the blessed Irenaeus, the martyr and bishop of Lyons, declares in his treatise *On Easter,* in which he makes mention of Pentecost also; upon which [feast] we do not bend the knee, because it is of equal significance with the Lord's day, for the reason already alleged concerning it.' ["Fragments from the Lost Writings of Irenaeus," 7] (*ANF* 1:569, 570).

"As the editors of the *Ante-Nicene Fathers* have observed, this reference must be to Easter. It seems clear that two *annual* events are intended; for Pentecost, an *annual event* is placed in comparison with 'Lord's day.'" —Strand, *The Sabbath in Scripture and History,* pp. 346–347, *except for mention of Clement, bracketed material in original.*

5. BARDAISAN (born 154):

"Wherever we be, all of us are called by the one name of the Messiah, namely Christians and upon one day which is the first day of the week we assemble ourselves together and on the appointed days we abstain from food."

FOCAL ISSUES: (1) time of writing and (2) non-biblical fast days.

Writing in the latter part of the second century, Bardaisan describes the solidification of Sunday assembly and the enactment of ceremonial appointed days not endorsed by Paul. In *Romans 14:5–6* (see **Q7** in back), Paul discusses the divisive nature of such elective fast days.

6. CYPRIAN, BISHOP OF CARTHAGE (200–258):

"The Lord's Day is both the first and the eighth day."

FOCAL ISSUE: Non-biblical argument of the "eighth day."

Cyprian simply reiterates the pseudo "eighth day" argument.

7. EUSEBIUS (*c.* 315):

"The churches throughout the rest of the world observe the practice that has prevailed from the Apostolic tradition until the present time so that it would not be proper to terminate our fast on any other day but the resurrection day of our Saviour. Hence, there were synods and convocations of our bishops on this question and they unanimously drew up an ecclesiastical decree which they communicated to churches in all places—that the mystery of the Lord's resurrection should be celebrated on no other than the Lord's day."

Constantine's influence reshaped the Church for many years to come.

FOCAL ISSUE: Eusebius wrote as a loyal supporter of the Sunday-worshipping Emperor Constantine.

Eusebius lived during the time that Constantine "converted" to Christianity without fully relinquishing sun worship. Eusebius was a high-ranking Church leader and historian who embraced and chronicled Constantine's involvement in the Church. It was during the time of Eusebius that the Catholic Church claims to have "transferred the solemnity" from the Sabbath to Sunday, echoing the Sunday law of Constantine of 321 A.D.

"We observe Sunday instead of Saturday because the Catholic church in the council of Laodicea (A.D. 338) transferred the solemnity from Saturday to Sunday." —Rev. Peter Geiermann, *The Catechism of Catholic Doctrine,* p. 50.

8. PETER, BISHOP OF ALEXANDRIA (*c.* 300):

"We keep the Lord's Day as a day of joy because of Him who arose thereon."

FOCAL ISSUES: (1) The time of writing and (2) the influence of Alexandria.

As a contemporary of Eusebius and Constantine (and as bishop of the city of *Alexandria)*, Bishop Peter's statement reflects the thinking of his contemporaries and of the anti-sabbatarian bias of his city.

9. DIDACHE (*teaching*) OF THE APOSTLES (*c.* 70–75):

"On the Lord's own day, gather yourselves together and break bread and give thanks."

FOCAL ISSUES: (1) Material date and (2) text mistranslation.

It is significant that Mr. Martin did not position this quotation earlier in his list, even though it purports to have been the "teaching of the Apostles." By placing it where he does, he quietly admits that, though parts of it may represent very early traditions, the majority of it is really not the "teaching of the Apostles."

"The *Didache,* a sort of baptismal, organizational, or instructional manual, has been dated anywhere from the late first century to the late second century, but scholarly opinion now favors a fairly early date, at least for a good deal of the material compiled in the *Didache.* The document seems to have originated in Syria.

"The statement in chapter 14 of interest here reads as follows: *Kata kuriakēn de kuriou sunachthentes klasate arton kai eucharistēsate*—'On the Lord's of the Lord [or, 'According to the Lord's of the Lord'] assemble, break bread, and hold Eucharist.' The word 'day' (Greek *hēmeran,* in the accusative case) does not actually appear in the text, but most translators have added it in their English translation, making the text read as follows: 'On the Lord's day. . . .' Some students of the text would, however, suggest the rendition 'According to the Lord's commandment. . .' also a possible translation of the original Greek. Samuele Bacchiocchi, following a rendition of

John Baptiste Thibaut and supporting it with a rather impressive line of evidence, gives a similar translation: 'According to the sovereign doctrine of the Lord.'" —Strand, *The Sabbath in Scripture and History,* pp. 347–348, *bracketed material in the original.*

In the verse before the one in question, we read: *arguriou de kai himatismou kai pantos ktematos labon ten aparchen hos an soi doxe, dos kata ten entolen*, which Lightfoot translates: "yea and of money and raiment and every possession take the first fruit, as shall seem good to thee, and give according to the commandment." The phrase, "according to the *commandment*," *kata ten entolen* (accusative singular), parallels the phrase at the beginning of the next verse: *kata kuriaken* (accusative singular) *de kuriou sunachthentes* (masculine plural participle). If the common phrasing in the two verses is used as a basis for translation, it would logically read: "When you gather together according to the sovereign *commandment* of the Lord. . ." and *not* "when you gather according to the Lord's *day* of the Lord." The context shows which supplied word makes more sense.

10. THE EPISTLE OF PLINY (to the Emperor Trajan, *c.* 112):

"They [the Christians] affirmed . . . that the whole of their crime or error was that they had been wont to meet together on a fixed day before daylight and to repeat among themselves in turn a hymn to Christ as to a god and to bind themselves by an oath (*sacramentum*) . . .; these things duly done, it had been their custom to disperse and to meet again to take food—of an ordinary and harmless kind. Even this they had ceased to do after my edict, by which, in accordance with your instructions, I had forbidden the existence of societies."

FOCAL ISSUE: Writing from outside the Church, Pliny appears to be describing an *annual* celebration rather than a weekly one.

"About A.D. 112 Pliny the Younger, governor of the province of Bithynia in northern Asia Minor, wrote a letter to Roman Emperor Trajan regarding the situation he met in dealing with Christians in his province. He indicates that he interrogated some former Christians who, under this questioning, indicated 'the whole of their guilt or their error' when they were Christians to have been that 'they were in the habit of meeting on a certain fixed day [*stato die*] before it was light, when they sang in alternate verses a hymn to Christ, as to a god, and bound themselves by a solemn oath, not to any wicked deeds, but never to commit any fraud, theft or adultery, never to falsify their word,' et cetera.

"In discussing this passage, Geraty points out that until the Jewish-Roman war of A.D. 132–135, the observance of a weekly day of worship would not, in Roman eyes, 'necessarily have involved guilt, but an annual vigil service in honor of the Lord's resurrection' might have done so. 'The Romans were used to, and permitted, the weekly religious rites of the Jews on their Sabbath, and possibly of pagan sun worshippers on their Sunday. However, now they had on their hands a new sect, the Christians, meeting on a *stato die ante lucem* and attributing divine honors to some person other than the Roman emperor; and this could certainly be looked upon as a danger to the Roman peace. Thus the reaction of the Romans, the time of meeting, and to a lesser degree the content of the service, would seem to indicate an Easter vigil celebration—if indeed earlier examples of this celebration were anything like what they later came to be.'"
—Strand, *The Sabbath in Scripture and History,* pp. 349, 350, *bracketed material in the original.*

Though not included in Walter Martin's list, the following quotation by Clement is here cited because it illustrates how important Greek philosophy was to the thinking of the Church Fathers.

11. CLEMENT (*c.* 190):

"The Lord's day Plato prophetically speaks of in the tenth book of the *Republic,* in these words: 'And when seven days have passed to each of them in the meadow, on the eighth they are to set out and arrive in four days.'"

FOCAL ISSUE: Appeal to extra-biblical source for support.

"The first Church Father whose extant writings use the term 'Lord's day' to apply to the weekly Christian Sunday was Clement of Alexandria near the close of the second century, probably about A.D. 190. Clement, who allegorized extensively in his theological discussions, thought that the Greek philosopher Plato some five and one-half centuries earlier had made a prophetic reference to Sunday. . . .

"Obviously, a future Christian Sunday . . . was totally foreign to Plato's mind . . ." —Strand, *The Sabbath in Scripture and History,* p. 346.

"Greek philosophy exercised the greatest influence . . . on the Christian mode of thought . . ." —Adolf von Harnack, *History of Dogma,* vol. I, p. 128.

All in all, the "Fathers" *are* a link of sorts, but not between Apostolic thought and later Church teaching, but between the Greek mode of thought and compromised Christianity.

"Christianity did not destroy paganism; it adopted it. The Greek mind, dying, came to a transmigrated life in the theology and liturgy of the Church; the Greek language, having reigned for centuries over philosophy, became the vehicle of Christian literature and ritual; the Greek mysteries passed down into the impressive mystery of the Mass. . . ." —Will Durant, *Caesar and Christ,* p. 595.

Now that we have examined the four major (and inherently conflicting) contemporary explanations for the abandonment of the Sabbath and have noted the conspicuous absence of direct apostolic testimony (in the New Testament) for its abandonment and (in the Fathers) for the exaltation of Sunday, it has become increasingly clear that the shift from Sabbath to Sunday worship was not an indisputable apostolic institution, but was the controversial innovation of a Church which had allowed itself to be willingly "hijacked" by the intellectual influences of the day.

As we continue our study, we will observe other covert agents that boarded that great vessel of spiritual truth, the Christian Church, commandeering it from its intended course of simple faith in the Word of God and taking it on a collision course with the twin towers of *human tradition* and *spiritual compromise.*

But, before we trace the Church's spiritually ill-fated course, let us go back in history to a dialogue that took place between Jesus and His disciples before the inception of Sunday observance.

6

From Sabbath day to "Lord's Day" in history

*I*nteracting with His disciples about the beautiful Jewish temple, one day, Jesus declared that the magnificent structure that they were beholding would soon be reduced to ruins. While the disciples were still reeling from this shocking revelation, Jesus also forewarned them that, with the appearance of the pagan ensign of the

Ruins of an ancient temple in Pella, city of refuge for the Nazarenes.

Roman armies in the precincts of Jerusalem, they were to flee from the city and, in anticipation of their departure, were to pray that their flight "be not in the winter," or "on the Sabbath day" (*Luke 21:20, 21; Matthew 24:15–20)*. In time, the disciples saw their Master's prediction fulfilled and, with the providential withdrawal of the Roman armies from

Jerusalem in 66 A.D., were able to flee across the Jordan to the safety of the little town of Pella in Perea, escaping the horrors that followed for those who remained behind until the return of the Romans in 70 A.D. These early disciples, known as *Nazarenes,* also prayed about and kept their Master's Sabbath, as their descendents (see **Q1** in back) and a great many other Christians continued to do for years to come—a fact which many historians candidly admit (although they also often assume that most early Christians also observed Sunday).

History reveals that all early Christians kept the Sabbath. "The first Christian church established at Jerusalem by apostolic authority became in its doctrine and practice a model for the greater part of those founded in the first century. . . . These Judaizing Christians were first known by the outside world as 'Nazarenes.' . . . All Christians agreed in celebrating the seventh day of the week in conformity to the Jewish converts." —Hugh Smith, *History of the Christian Church,* pp. 50, 51, 69.

". . . The church [of Jerusalem] moved to Pella, a Gentile city east of the Jordan, and there survived for a time. Some of the Jewish Christians, referred to by one or more early Christian writers as Nazarenes, held that Jesus was the Messiah, the Son of God, and that his teachings are superior to those of Moses and the prophets, but that Christians of Jewish descent should observe the Jewish laws of circumcision, Sabbath observance, and foods. . . ." —Latourette, *A History of Christianity,* vol. 1, p. 121. (Nonetheless, other historic evidence indicates that Sabbath observance was not limited to Christians of Jewish descent alone. The continued observance of the Sabbath in the churches of Egypt, India, Abyssinia and other eastern cities indicates that the Sabbath was taken wherever the early missionaries carried the gospel. See Mark Finley, *The Almost Forgotten Day,* pp. 62–65.)

Even heathen converts observed the Sabbath. "While the Jewish Christians of Palestine, who kept the whole Jewish law, celebrated of course all the Jewish festivals, the heathen converts observed only the Sabbath, and, in remembrance of the closing scenes of our Saviour's life, the Passover, though without the Jewish superstitions. Besides these, the Sunday, as the day of our Saviour's resurrection, was devoted to religious worship" —Gieseler, *"Apostolic Age to A.D. 70," A Text-book of Church History,* Section 29.

But soon the religions of polytheism overwhelmed the Nazarenes. ". . . The Jewish converts, or, as they were afterwards called, the Nazarenes, who had laid the foundations of the church, soon found themselves overwhelmed by the increasing multitudes, that from all the various religions of polytheism enlisted under the banner of Christ: . . . The Nazarenes retired from the ruins of Jerusalem to a little town of Pella beyond Jordan, where that ancient church languished above sixty years in solitude and obscurity." —Edward Gibbon, *The Decline and Fall of the Roman Empire,* vol. 1, chap. 15, p. 387.

50 years after Paul, a different Church emerges. "For fifty years after St. Paul's life a curtain hangs over the church, through which we vainly strive to look; and when at last the curtain rises, about 120 A.D. with the writings of the earliest church-fathers, we find a church in many aspects very different from that in the days of St. Peter and St. Paul."—Jesse L. Hurlbut, *The Story of the Christian Church,* p. 41.

Changes in the Church were predicted by Paul. Paul, who was seen as "a ring-leader of the sect of the Nazarenes" (*Acts 24:5*) because he—with the Nazarenes—observed the Sabbath (*Acts 13:14, 42, 44; 16:13; 17:2; 18:4*) and believed Jesus to be the Messiah, warned about the influence on believers of the "philosophy . . . [and] rudiments of this world" (*Colossians 2:8).* He warned about those who would attack and plunder the Church (*Acts 20:29, 30)* and about a great "falling away" from the truth, linked with the revealing of the "son of perdition" (a term used, in *John 17:2,* to describe Judas, the betraying "insider"), under the influence of the "mystery of iniquity"—that secretive power that would set itself against the law of God. (For more on this topic, see the book, *Truth Left Behind,* listed in "*For further study*.")

"Let no man deceive you by any means: for that day shall not come, except there come a falling away [Gr. apostasia] first, and that man of sin be revealed, the son of perdition; [7] *For the mystery of iniquity [Gr. anomia, "lawlessness."] doth already work: only he who now letteth will let, until he be taken out of the way.* [8] *And then shall that Wicked be revealed, whom the Lord shall consume with the spirit of his mouth, and shall destroy with the brightness of his coming:* [9] *Even him, whose coming is after the working of Satan with all power and signs and lying wonders,* [10] *And with all deceivableness of unrighteousness in them that perish; because they received not the love of the truth, that they might be saved." 2 Thessalonians 2:3, 7–10.*

By the middle of the second century, the Church had seen great changes. "Before the second century was half gone, before the last of the apostles had been dead forty years, this apostate, this working of the mystery of iniquity, had so largely spread over the East and the West, that it is literally true, that 'a large part of the Christian observances and institutions, even in this century, had the aspect of the pagan mysteries' [Mosheim, *Ecclesiastical History,* Century 2, Part 2, Chapter 4, Paragraph 1] —Alonzo T. Jones, *The Great Empires of Prophecy From Babylon to the Fall of Rome, chap. XXVI, p. 381.*

Sunday arose as Christians sought to distinguish themselves from the Jews. "Our investigation . . . has established that Sunday observance arose, as W. D. Davies states, 'in conscious opposition to or distinction from the Jewish Sabbath.' [W. D. Davies, *Christian Origins and Judaism,* n.d., p. 74.] We have found that the change in the day of worship seems to have been encouraged, on the one hand, by the social, military, political and literary anti-Judaic imperial policies which made it necessary for Christians to sever their ties with the Jews, and, on the other hand, by the very conflict existing between Jews and Christians. The Church of Rome, whose members, mostly of pagan extraction, experienced a break from the Jews earlier than in the East and where the unpopularity of the Jews was particularly great, appears to have played a leading role in inducing the adoption of Sunday observance. This we found indicated not only by the introduction and enforcement of the new Easter-Sunday festivity (closely related to the weekly Sunday) but also by the measures Rome took to devaluate the Sabbath theologically and practically. The Sabbath was in fact re-interpreted to be a temporary institution given to the Jews as a sign of their unfaithfulness. Therefore Christians were enjoined to show their dissociation from the Jewish Sabbath by fasting on that day, by abstaining from the Lord's supper and by not attending religious assemblies." —***Samuele Bacchiocchi*** (first non-Catholic to graduate from the Pontifical Gregorian University in Rome, author and retired professor of theology and church history), *From Sabbath to Sunday,* p. 212.

Sunday at first supplemental to the Sabbath. "The observance of the Sunday was at first supplemental to that of the Sabbath, but in proportion as the gulf between the Church and the Synagogue widened, the Sabbath became less and less important, and ended at length in being entirely neglected (Duchesne, *Christian Worship,* 47)." —Bertrand L. Conway ([1872–1959] Paulist father in the *Catholic Church), The Question Box,* 1960, p. 410.

Both days kept by the early church, but Sabbath was observed after the spiritual manner. ". . . The primitive Christians did keep the sabbath of the Jews . . . At first they kept both days, with this only difference, that though they kept the sabbath, yet it was after the christian, that is, after the spiritual manner. . . ." —Bishop Jeremy Taylor (*Church of England), The Rule of Conscience,* 1851, p. 456, 457.

"We have seen how gradually the impression of the Jewish sabbath faded from the mind of the Christian church, and how completely the newer thought underlying the observance of the first day took possession of the church. We have seen that the Christian of the first three centuries never confused one with the other, but for a time celebrated both." —*The Sunday Problem (Lutheran)*, 1923, p. 36.

Sabbath observance maintained in the Eastern Churches. "The ancient Sabbath did remain and was observed together with the celebration of the Lord's day by the Christians of the east church above three hundred years after our Saviour's death. That church being the great part of Christendom, and having the apostles' doctrine and example to instruct them, would have restrained it if it had been deadly." —Edward Brerewood (professor in Gresham College, London), *A Learned Treatise of the Sabbath*, Oxford, *1631*, p. 77.

"The ancient Christians were very careful in the observance of Saturday, or the seventh day . . . It is plain that all the Oriental churches, and the greatest part of the world, observed the Sabbath as a festival . . . Athanasius likewise tells us that they held religious assembles on the Sabbath, not because they were infected with Judaism, but to worship Jesus, the Lord of the Sabbath, Epiphanius says the same." —*Antiquities of the Christian Church*, Vol. II Book XX, chap. 3, sec. 1, 66. 1137, 1138.

". . . In many of the Oriental churches the Sabbath (Saturday) was still observed like Sunday, while in the West a large number, by way of opposition to Jewish institutions, held a fast on that day." —George Park Fisher ([1827–1909] professor of ecclesiastical history at Yale University), *History of the Christian Church*, p. 118.

"By the second half of the fourth century, the practice of keeping both Sabbath and Sunday was widespread in Christian Asia, as witnessed by several documents. For example, the so-called *Constitutions of the Holy Apostles,* composed in Syria *c.* A.D. 375, reflect what probably was the generalized attitude toward Sabbath-Sunday observance in the Eastern Church at that time: 'But keep the Sabbath, and the Lord's day festival; because the former is the memorial of the creation, and the latter of the resurrection.'" —Werner K. Vyhmeister "The Sabbath in Asia," *The Sabbath in Scripture and History*, 1982, p. 151.

Until the second century, Sunday was a regular work day. "The keeping of the Sunday rest arose from the custom of the people and the constitution of the Church. . . . Tertullian [*c.* 155– *c.* 225 A.D.] was probably the first to refer to a cessation of worldly affairs on the Sunday; the Council of Laodicea [4th century] issued the first conciliar legislation for that day; Constantine I issued the first civil legislation." —Priest Vincent J. Kelly, *Forbidden Sunday and Feast-Day Occupations* [a thesis presented to the Catholic University of America], p. 203.

Christians of Rome and Alexandria did not assemble on the Sabbath. "The people of Constantinople, and almost everywhere, assemble together on the Sabbath, as well as on the first day of the week, which custom is never observed at Rome or at Alexandria." —Hermias Sozomen, *Ecclesiastical History,* bk. 7, chap. 19 [written *c.* 460 A.D.].

"Although almost all churches throughout the world celebrate the sacred mysteries on the Sabbath every week, yet the Christians of Alexandria and at Rome, on account of some ancient tradition, have ceased [another translation has "refuse"] to do this." —Socrates Scholasticus, *Ecclesiastical History,* Book 5, chap. 22, p. 289 [*c.* 439 A.D.].

Rome played a key role in the abandonment of the Sabbath. "The role that the Church of Rome played in causing the abandonment of the Sabbath and the adoption of Sunday has been underestimated, if not totally neglected, in recent studies. . . . It is there that we found both the circumstances and the authority necessary to accomplish such a liturgical change. . . . C. S. Mosna specifically admits that Rome was influential in causing the disappearance of the veneration of the Sabbath. He states, 'perhaps in this the example of Rome, which never had any special cult on the Sabbath, must have been influential.' [Mosna, p. 354.] These conditions did not exist in the East where Jewish influence survived longer, as evidenced by the survival of a veneration for the Sabbath and of respect for the Jewish reckoning of the Passover. [*Footnote:* "Bruce Metzger acknowledges that the need for Christians in the West to separate from the Jews provides 'a reasonable historical explanation' for 'the difference between East and West in the observance of the Sabbath. . . . In the West, particularly after the Jewish rebellion under Hadrian, it became vitally important for those who were not Jews to avoid exposing themselves to suspicion; and the observance of the Sabbath was one of the most noticeable indications of Judaism. In the East, however, less opposition was shown to Jewish institutions' *(Studies in the Lectionary Text of the Greek New Testament,* 1944, II, sec. 3, p. 12)."]" —Bacchiocchi, *From Sabbath to Sunday,* pp. 211, 212.

Gentile Christians of Rome and Alexandria were prone to accept worship on the Sunday "Lord's Day." "As we have already noted, excepting for the Roman and Alexandrian Christians, the majority of Christians were observing the seventh-day Sabbath at least as late as the middle of the fifth century [*c.* 450 A.D.]. The Roman and Alexandrian Christians were among those converted from heathenism. They began observing Sunday as a merry religious festival in honor of the Lord's resurrection, about the latter half of the second century A.D. However, they did not try to teach that the Lord or His apostles commanded it. In fact, no ecclesiastical writer before Eusebius of Caesarea in the fourth century even suggested that either Christ or His apostles instituted the observance of the first day of the week.

"These Gentile Christians of Rome and Alexandria began calling the first day of the week 'the Lord's day.' This was not difficult for the pagans of the Roman Empire who were steeped in sun worship to accept, because they referred to their sun-god as their 'Lord.'" —E. M. Chalmers, *How Sunday Came Into the Christian Church,* p. 3.

Sunday adopted to attract the Gentiles. "The Gentiles were an idolatrous people who worshipped the sun, and Sunday was their most sacred day. Now in order to reach the people in this new field, it seems natural as well as necessary to make Sunday the rest day of the Church. At this time, it was necessary for the church to either adopt the Gentiles' day or else have the Gentiles change their day. To change the Gentiles' day would have been a stumbling block and an offense to them. The church would naturally reach them better by keeping their day. There was no need in causing an unnecessary offense by dishonoring their day." —Rev. William Frederick, *Sunday and the Christian Sabbath,* pp. 169, 170 (quoted in *Signs of the Times,* September 6, 1927).

The sun cult was supreme in Rome. "Sun worship was the earliest idolatry (Job xxxi. 26, 27) . . ." —A. R. Fausset, *Bible Dictionary,* p. 666. It was also "one of the oldest components of the Roman religion." —Gaston H. Halsberghe, *The Cult of Sol Invictus [the unconquered sun],* 1972, p. 26.

"The solar theology of the 'Chaldaeans' [i.e., "the Babylonian priests of the Hellenistic age"] had a decisive effect upon the final development of Semitic paganism . . . [The educated priesthood of Syria] followed them [the Chaldeans] in seeing the sun the directing power of the cosmic system. All the Baals were thence forward turned into suns, the sun being the mover of the other stars, like it eternal and 'unconquerable.' . . . Such was the final form reached by the religion of the pagan Semites, and, following them, by that of the Romans . . . when they raised *Sol invictus* to the rank of supreme divinity in the Empire." —Franz F. V. M. Cumont, *The Cambridge Ancient History,* vol. 11, pp. 643, 646–647.

Sol, sun god of Mithraism

"Remains of the struggle [between Christianity and Mithraism—the Roman Sun cult] are found in two institutions adopted from its rival by Christianity in the fourth century, the two Mithraic sacred days: December twenty-fifth, *dies natalis solis* [birthday of the sun], as the birthday of Jesus, and Sunday, 'the venerable day of the Sun,' as Constantine called it in his edict of 321." —Walter Woodburn Hyde, *Paganism to Christianity in the Roman Empire,* 1946, p. 60.

Sunday was observed to keep from hindering the conversion of the Gentiles. "Sunday being the first day of which the Gentiles solemnly adored that planet and called it Sunday, partly from its influence on that day especially, and partly in respect to its divine body (as they conceived it) the Christians thought fit to keep the same day and the same name of it, that they might not appear carelessly peevish, and by that means hinder the conversion of the Gentiles, and bring a greater prejudice that might be otherwise taken against the gospel." —T. M. Morer (*Presbyterian*), *Dialogues on the Lord's Day,* 1701, p. 23.

FIDES (faith) with cross, cup and pagan sunburst

Paganism and Christianity, at first in conflict, tended to merge. "From simple beginning, the church developed a distinct priesthood and an elaborate service. In this way, Christianity and the higher forms of paganism tended to come nearer and nearer to each other as time went on. In one sense, it is true, they met like armies in mortal conflict, but at the same time they tended to merge into one another like streams which had been following converging courses." —J. H. Robinson, *Introduction to the History of Western Europe,* p. 30.

Corruptions early crept into the Church. "There is scarcely anything which strikes the mind of the careful student of ancient ecclesiastical history with greater surprise than the comparatively early period at which many of the corruptions of Christianity, which are embodied in the Roman system, took their rise; yet it is not to be supposed that when the first originators of many of these unscriptural notions and practices planted those germs of corruption, they anticipated or even imagined they would ever grow into such a vast and hideous system of superstition and error as is that of popery." —John Dowling, *History of Romanism,* 13th Edition, p. 65.

"... when the heathen converts were received in the church, it was natural they should bring with them some taint of their old philosophy, and former superstitions; and some fondness for the rites and ceremonies of their idolatrous worship. ... Indeed we shall find, that when Christianity became the established religion of the Roman Empire, and took the place of paganism, it assumed, in a great degree, the forms and

"La Verita" (Truth), embracing the sun; part of a sculpture at St. Peter's in Rome

rites of paganism, and participated in no small measure of its spirit also. Christianity as it existed in the dark ages, might be termed, without much impropriety of language, baptized paganism." —James Wharey, *Sketches of Church History* (Presbyterian Board of Publications, 1840), p. 23.

"In the interval between the days of the apostles and the conversion of Constantine, the Christian commonwealth changed it[s] aspect. The Bishop of Rome—a personage unknown to the writers of the New Testament—meanwhile rose into prominence, and at length took precedence of all other churchmen. Rites and ceremonies, of which neither Paul nor Peter ever heard, crept silently into use, and then claimed the rank of Divine institutions. Officers for whom the primitive disciples could have found no place, and titles, which to them would have been altogether unintelligible, began to challenge attention, and to be named apostolic." —William D. Killen, *The Ancient Church,* pp. xv, xvi.

Sunday united pagans and Christians. "The retention of the old pagan name of '*Dies Solis,*' or 'Sunday,' for the weekly Christian festival, is, in great measure, owing to the union of pagan and Christian sentiment with which the first day of the week was recommended by Constantine to his subjects Pagan and Christian alike, as the 'venerable day of the sun' . . . It was his mode of harmonizing the discordant religions of the Empire under one common institution." —Dean Stanley, *Lectures on the Eastern Church,* Lecture 6, p. 184.

The Church absorbed pagan practices. ". . . In the course of the fourth century two movements or developments spread over the face of Christendom, with a rapidity characteristic of the Church; the one ascetic, the other ritual or ceremonial. We are told in various ways by Eusebius [*V. Const.* iii. 1, iv. 23, &c.], that Constantine, in order to recommend the new religion to the heathen, transferred into it the outward ornaments to which they had been accustomed in their own. It is not necessary to go into a subject which the diligence of Protestant writers has made familiar to most of us. The use of temples, and these dedicated to particular saints, and ornamented on occasions with branches of trees; incense, lamps, and candles; votive offerings on recovery from illness; holy water; asylums; holydays and seasons, use of calendars, processions, blessings on the fields; sacerdotal vestments, the tonsure, the ring in marriage, turning to the

 East, images at a later date, perhaps the ecclesiastical chant, and the Kyrie Eleison, are all of pagan origin, and sanctified by their adoption into the Church." —*Cardinal John Henry Newman* ([1801–1890) Anglican cleric who led out in the "Oxford Movement" [1833–1841]—a movement to bring Roman Catholic ritualism back into the Anglican

Church—writing shortly before he became a Roman Catholic and was subsequently ordained a cardinal), *An Essay on the Development of Christian Doctrine,* 1845, p. 373.

"The Church took the pagan philosophy and made it the buckler of faith against the heathen. She took the pagan Roman Pantheon, temple to all the gods, and made it sacred to all the martyrs; so it stands to this day. She took the pagan Sunday and made it the Christian Sunday . . . The Sun was a foremost god with heathendom. Balder the beautiful, the White God, the old Scandinavians called him. The sun has worshipers at this

Of Constantine's ostensible conversion, Eusebius wrote: "He said that about noon, when the day was already beginning to decline, he saw with his own eyes the trophy of a cross of light in the heavens, above the sun, and bearing the inscription, 'Conquer by this.' At this sight he himself was struck with amazement, and his whole army also, which followed him on this expedition, and witnessed the miracle." (Eusebius, Life of Constantine 1:28), emphasis supplied.

very hour in Persia and other lands. . . . There is, in truth, something royal, kingly about the sun, making it a fit emblem of Jesus, the Sun of Justice. Hence the Church would seem to have said, 'Keep that old, pagan name. It shall remain consecrated, sanctified.' And thus the pagan Sunday, dedicated to Balder, became the Christian Sunday, sacred to Jesus. The sun is a fitting emblem of Jesus. The Fathers often compared Jesus to the sun; as they compared Mary to the moon . . ."
—William L. Gildea, "Paschale Gaudium," in *The Catholic World,* 58 (March, 1894), p. 809.

Christian emperors did not forsake their roots in sun worship.
"With Constantius Cholorus [Constantine's father] (A.D. 305) there ascended the throne [of the Roman Empire] a solar dynasty which . . . professed to have Sol Invictus as its special protector and ancestor. Even the Christian emperors, Constantine and Constantius, did not altogether forget the pretensions which they could derive from so illustrious a descent . . ." —Franz F. V. M. Cumont, *Astrology and Religion Among the Greeks and Romans,* 1960, p. 55.

Part of the old passes into the new. "When Christianity conquered Rome, the ecclesiastical structure of the pagan church, the title and the vestments of the *pontifex maximus,* the worship of the Great Mother goddess and a multitude of comforting divinities, . . . the joy or solemnity of old festivals, and the pageantry of immemorial ceremony, passed like maternal blood into the new religion, and captive Rome conquered her conqueror. The reins and skills of government were handed down by a dying empire to a virile papacy." —Will Durant, *Caesar and Christ,* pp. 671, 672.

"The power of the Caesars lived again in the universal dominion of the popes." —H. G. Guinness, *Romanism and the Reformation,* lecture 4.

Constantine's Sunday law. "On the venerable Day of the Sun [*venerabili die Solis*—the sacred day of the Sun] let the magistrates and people residing in cities rest, and let all workshops be closed. In the country, however, persons engaged in agriculture may freely and lawfully continue their pursuits; because it often happens that another day is not so suitable for grain-sowing or for vine-planting; lest by neglecting the proper moment for such operations the bounty of heaven should be lost. (Given the 7th day of March, Crispus and Constantine being consuls each of them for the second time.)" —*Codex Justinianus*.

Church and State union and Sunday legislation. "This is the 'parent' Sunday law making it a day of rest and release from labor. For from that time to the present there have been decrees about the observance of Sunday which have profoundly influenced European and American society. When the Church became a part of State under the Christian emperors, Sunday observance was enforced by civil statutes, and later when the Empire was past, the Church in the hands of the papacy enforced it by ecclesiastical, and also influenced it by civil enactments." —Walter W. Hyde, *Paganism to Christianity in the Roman Empire,* 1946, p. 261.

Constantine sought to make one religion of paganism and Christianity. "Constantine labored at this time untiringly to unite the worshipers of the old and the new into one religion. All his laws and contrivances are aimed at promoting this amalgamation of religions. He would by all lawful and peaceable means melt together a purified heathenism and moderated Christianity. . . . His injunction that the

'Day of the Sun' should be a general rest day was characteristic of his standpoint. . . . Of all his blending and melting together of Christianity and heathenism none is more easy to see through than this making of his Sunday law. The Christians worshipped their Christ, the heathen their sun-god; according to the opinion of the Emperor, the objects for worship in both religions were essentially the same." —H. G. Heggtveit, *Illustreret Kirkehistorie,* 1895, p. 202.

Constantine's edict is followed by a series of Church injunctions against the Sabbath. "Constantine's decree marked the beginning of a long, though intermittent series of imperial decrees in support of Sunday rest." —Vincent J. Kelly, *Forbidden Sunday and Feast-Day Occupations,* 1943, p. 29.

First Sunday Law decree of a Christian council. "Christians shall not Judaize and be idle on Saturday [Greek *sabbaton,* "Sabbath"] but shall work on that day; but the Lord's day they shall especially honour, and, as being Christians, shall, if possible, do no work on that day. If, however, they are found Judaizing, they shall be shut out [*anathema*] from Christ." —*Council of Laodicea,* c. A.D. 337, canon 29, translated in C. J. Hefele, *A History of the Christian Councils,* Vol. 2, p. 316.

Subsequent depreciation of the Sabbath. "All things whatsoever that was duty to do on the Sabbath, these we [the Church] have transferred them to the Lord's day, as being more authoritative and more highly regarded and first in rank, and more honorable than the Jewish Sabbath." —Bishop Eusebius, *Commentary on the Psalms,* on Ps. 91 (92): 2, 3.

"If every Sunday is to be observed joyfully by the Christians on account of the resurrection, then every Sabbath on account of the burial is to be regarded in execration [cursing] of the Jews." —Pope Sylvester ([314–337) is said to have baptized Constantine shortly before his death), quoted by S. R. E. Humbert, *Adversus Graecorum Calumnias,* in J. -P. Migne, *Patrologia Graeca,* p. 143.

"About 590, Pope Gregory, in a letter to the Roman people, denounced as the prophets of Antichrist those who maintained that work ought not to be done on the seventh day." —James T. Ringgold, *The Law of Sunday,* p. 267.

Sabbath observance gradually diminishes. "Down even to the fifth century the observance of the Jewish Sabbath was continued in the Christian church, but with a rigor and solemnity gradually diminishing until it was wholly discontinued." —Lyman Coleman, *Ancient Christianity Exemplified,* chap. 26, sec. 2, p. 527. (However, *The Almost Forgotten Day,* pp. 60–93, documents that Sabbath keeping continued among Christians outside the direct shadow of Rome.)

From pagan ordinance to Christian regulation. "The earliest Sunday law, the edict issued by Constantine in 321 A.D., bore no relation to Christianity. What began, however, as a pagan ordinance, ended as a Christian regulation; and a long series of imperial decrees, during the fourth, fifth, and sixth centuries, enjoined with increasing stringency abstinence from labor on Sunday." —Hutton Webster, *Rest Days,* 1916, p. 270.

What authority do Church leaders claim for Sunday worship? Scriptural authority or Church tradition?

7

Protestants, Catholics, and the authority for Sunday worship

*S*cripture is not the source of the change. "Sunday is a Catholic institution, and its claims to observance can be defended only on Catholic principles . . . From beginning to end of scripture there is not a single page that warrants the transfer of weekly public worship from the last day of the week to the first." —*Catholic Press,* Sydney, Australia, August, 1900.

". . . is not every Christian obliged to sanctify Sunday and to abstain on that day from unnecessary servile work? Is not the observance of this law among the most prominent of our sacred duties? But you may read the Bible from Genesis to Revelation, and you will not find a single line authorizing the sanctification of Sunday. The Scriptures enforce the religious observance of Saturday, a day which we never sanctify. . . . We must therefore conclude that the Scriptures alone cannot be a sufficient guide and rule of faith." —*James Cardinal Gibbons* ([1834–1921] archbishop of Baltimore and principal leader of American Catholicism during the period of its greatest growth, whose leadership helped to achieve integration of Roman Catholicism into American society), *The Faith of Our Fathers,* pp. 80.

No such law in the Bible. "All of us believe many things in regard to religion that we do not find in the Bible. For example, nowhere in the Bible do we find that Christ or the Apostles ordered that the Sabbath be changed from Saturday to Sunday. We have the commandment of God given to Moses to keep holy the Sabbath Day, that is the 7th day of the week, Saturday. Today most Christians keep Sunday because it has been revealed to us by the Church outside the Bible." —"To Tell You The Truth," *The Catholic Virginian,* vol. 22 (Oct. 3, 1947), no. 49.

Church claims prerogative of God in granting men rest. Not the Creator of the Universe, in Genesis 2:1–3, but the Catholic Church "can claim the honor of having granted man a pause to his work every seven days." —Corrado S. Mosna, *Storia della Domenica dalle origini fino agli Inizi del V Secolo,* 1969, pp. 366–367.

The Sunday institution is purely a creation of the Catholic Church. "The Sunday, as a day of the week set apart for the obligatory public worship of Almighty God, to be sanctified by a suspension of all servile labor, trade, and worldly avocations and by exercises of devotion, is purely a creation of the Catholic Church." —John Gilmary Shea ([1824–1892) an important Catholic historian of his time), *The American Catholic Quarterly Review,* January, 1883, p. 139.

The Church claims the change was made by its divine mission. "The Catholic Church for over one thousand years before the existence of a Protestant, by virtue of her divine mission, changed the day from Saturday to Sunday." —*The Christian Sabbath,* p. 29.

Sunday is proof of the Church's power to change law. ". . . The Sabbath, the most glorious day in the law, has been changed into the Lord's day. . . by the authority of the church. . . ." —Gaspare [Ricciulli] de Fosso (Archbishop of Reggio), Address in the 17th session of the Council of Trent (the Council of Trent was convened in response to the Reformation), Jan. 18, 1562, in Mansi, *Sacrorum Conciliorum,* vol. 33, cols. 529, 530. Latin

"Question. How prove you that the Church hath power to command feasts and holydays?

"Answer. By the very act of changing the Sabbath into Sunday, which Protestants allow of [by observing it]; and therefore they fondly contradict themselves, by keeping Sunday strictly, and breaking most other feasts commanded by the same church." —Priest Henry Tuberville (received a papal approbation for this book in 1833), *An Abridgement of the Christian Doctrine,* p. 58.

The Church claims divine power to abolish Sabbath and to command to keep Sunday. "Prove to me from the Bible alone that I am bound to keep Sunday holy. There is no such law in the Bible. It is a law of the holy Catholic Church alone. The Bible says 'Remember the Sabbath day to keep it holy.' The Catholic Church says, 'No. By my divine power I abolish the Sabbath day and command you to keep holy the first day of the week.' And lo! The entire civilized world bows down in reverent obedience to the command of the Holy Catholic Church." —Priest Thomas Enright, CSSR, President of Redemptorist College, Kansas City, Missouri, in a lecture at Hartford, Kansas, February 18, 1884, and the *American Sentinel* (a New York Roman Catholic journal), June 1893, p. 173.

The Church claims to have changed the commandment. "They [the Catholics] allege the change of the Sabbath into the Lord's day, contrary, as it seemeth, to the Decalogue; and they have no example more in their mouths than the change of the Sabbath. They will needs have the Church's power to be very great, because it hath dispensed with a precept of the Decalogue." —*The Augsburg Confession* (written by Melanchthon in 1530, 13 years after Luther wrote his 95 theses), part 2, art. 7, "Of Ecclesiastical Power."

Change a mark of the Church's power. "Of course the Catholic Church claims that the change [of the Sabbath to Sunday] was her act ... and the act is *a mark of her ecclesiastical power.*" —H. F. Thomas, chancellor for James Cardinal Gibbons, November 11, 1895, *emphasis supplied.*

Sunday shows the Church's authority. "The Church is above the Bible: and this transference of Sabbath observance is proof of that fact. Deny the authority of the Church and you have no adequate or reasonable explanation or justification for the substitution of Sunday for Saturday in the Third—Protestant Fourth—Commandment of God. . . ."—*The Catholic Record* of London, Ontario, Canada, Sept. 1, 1923.

"36. *The Sunday assembly* is the privileged place of unity: it is the setting for the celebration of the *sacramentum unitatis* which profoundly *marks* the Church as a people gathered 'by' and 'in' the unity of the Father, of the Son and of the Holy Spirit.(49) For Christian families, the Sunday assembly is one of the most outstanding expressions of their identity and their 'ministry' as 'domestic churches,'(50) when parents share with their children at the one Table of the word and of the Bread of Life. We do well to recall in this regard that it is first of all the parents who must teach their children to participate in Sunday Mass; they are assisted in this by catechists,

who are to see to it that initiation into the Mass is made a part of the formation imparted to the children entrusted to their care, explaining the important reasons behind the obligatory nature of the precept."
—Pope John Paul II, *Dies Domini,* May 31, 1998, *emphasis supplied.*

Change of Sunday is proof of the Church's authority. "Q. Have you any other way of proving that the Church has power to institute festivals of precept?

"A. Had she no such power, she could not have done that in which all modern religionists agree with her;—she could not have substituted the observance of Sunday the first day of the week, for the observance of Saturday the seventh day, a change for which there is no Scriptural authority." —Rev. Stephen Keenan, *A Doctrinal Catechism,* 1876, p. 174.

The Church claims divine authority in making the change. "The Church changed the observance of the Sabbath to Sunday by right of the divine, infallible authority given to her by her Founder, Jesus Christ. The Protestant, claiming the Bible to be the only guide of faith, has no warrant for observing Sunday. In this matter the Seventh Day Adventist is the only consistent Protestant. Sunday as the day of rest to honor our Lord's Resurrection dates to Apostolic times and was so established among other reasons, to mark off the Jew from the Christian. St. Justin the Martyr, speaks of it in his Apologies."
—"The Question Box," *The Catholic Universe Bulletin,* 69 (August 14, 1942), p. 4.

Without Catholic authority, Protestants have no good reasons for Sunday observance. ". . . Protestantism, in discarding the authority of the [Roman Catholic] Church, has no good reason for its Sunday theory, and ought, logically, to keep Saturday as the Sabbath, with the Jews and the seventh-day Baptists. For their present practice Protestants in general have no authority but that of a Church which they disown, and there cannot be a greater inconsistency than theirs in asking the state to enforce the Sunday laws." —John Gilmary Shea, *The American Catholic Quarterly Review,* 8 (January, 1883), p. 152.

Martin Luther articulated the Protestant teaching of Sola Scriptura which takes the Bible as the only rule of faith and practice.

Church demonstrated *sense* **"of its own authority" by changing day of worship to Sunday.** "The Church has always had a strong sense of its own authority 'Whatever you bind on earth is bound in heaven,' Jesus said.

"Perhaps the boldest thing, the most revolutionary change the church ever did, happened in the first century. The holy day, the Sabbath, was changed from Saturday to Sunday. 'The Day of the Lord' (*dies Dominica*) was chosen, not from any directions noted in the Scriptures, but from the Church's sense of its own power. The day of resurrection, the day of Pentecost, fifty days later, came on the first day of the week. So this would be the new Sabbath. People who think that the Scriptures should be the sole authority, should logically become 7th Day Adventists, and keep Saturday holy." —*Sentinel* (newsletter published by the Saint Catherine Catholic Church of Algonac, Michigan), May 21, 1995.

Christians *felt* **they had the authority**. "63. Christ came to accomplish a new 'exodus,' to restore freedom to the oppressed. He performed many healings on the Sabbath (cf. Mt 12:9–14 and parallels), certainly not to violate the Lord's Day, but to reveal its full meaning: 'The Sabbath was made for man, not man for the Sabbath' (Mk 2:27). Opposing the excessively legalistic interpretation of some of his contemporaries, and developing the true meaning of the biblical Sabbath, Jesus, as 'Lord of the Sabbath' (Mk 2:28), restores to the Sabbath observance its liberating character, carefully safeguarding the rights of God and the rights of man. This is why Christians, called as they are to proclaim the liberation won by the blood of Christ, felt that they had the authority to transfer the meaning of the Sabbath to the day of the Resurrection." —Pope John Paul II, *Dies Domini.*

Some teachings are carried on the strength of tradition. "Some of the truths that have been handed down to us by Tradition and are not recorded in the Sacred Scriptures, are the following: that there are just seven Sacraments; that there is a Purgatory; that, in the New Law, Sunday should be kept holy instead of the Sabbath; that infants should be baptized, and that there are precisely seventy-two books in the Bible [the 66 accepted as inspired by Protestants, plus six apocryphal books accepted by Rome]." —Francis J. Butler ([1859–?] Catholic priest of Boston and author of a series of catechisms), *Holy Family Series of Catholic Catechisms,* p. 63.

The Church chose Sunday. "Some theologians have held that God likewise directly determined the Sunday as the day of worship in the

New Law, that He Himself has explicitly substituted the Sunday for the Sabbath. But this theory is now entirely abandoned. It is now commonly held that God simply gave His Church the power to set aside whatever day or days, she would deem suitable as Holy Days. The Church chose Sunday, the first day of the week, and in the course of time added other days, as holy days." —Vincent J. Kelly, *Forbidden Sunday and Feast-Day Occupations,* 1943, p. 2.

The Bible and Tradition are equally sacred for the Catholic. "Like two sacred rivers flowing from Paradise, the Bible and divine Tradition contain the Word of God, the precious gems of revealed truth.

"Though these two divine streams are in themselves, on account of their divine origin, of equal sacredness, and are both full of revealed truths, still, of the two, TRADITION is to us more clear and safe." —Joseph Faà di Bruno, *Catholic Belief,* 1884, p. 45.

The Christian must either follow the Bible or Catholic tradition. "Reason and common sense demand the acceptance of one or the other of these alternatives: either Protestantism and the keeping holy of Saturday, or Catholicity and the keeping of Sunday. *Compromise is impossible.*" —Abram Herbert Lewis, D.D., "Catholic Proof," *Catholic Mirror,* Dec. 23, 1893.

If the Bible is the only guide, then Christians should worship on Saturday. "What Bible authority is there for changing the Sabbath from the seventh to the first day of the week?

"Who gave the Pope the authority to change a command of God?

"If the Bible is the only guide for the Christian, then the Seventh Day Adventist is right in observing the Saturday with the Jew. But Catholics learn what to believe and do from the divine, infallible authority established by Jesus Christ, the Catholic Church, which in Apostolic times made Sunday the day of rest to honor our Lord's resurrection on that day, and to mark off clearly the Jew from the Christian. St. Justin Martyr (Apol., c. 67) speaks of the early Christians meeting for the holy sacrifice of the Mass on Sunday.

"Is it not strange that those who make the Bible their only teacher should inconsistently follow in this matter the tradition of the Church?" —Bertrand L. Conway, *The Question-Box Answers,* 1910, pp. 254, 255.

What does it mean if we accept tradition over biblical authority?

8

The acceptance of Church tradition over biblical authority

*I*n keeping Sunday, Protestants are following a law of the Catholic Church. "If Protestants would follow the Bible, they should worship God on the Sabbath Day. In keeping the Sunday they are following a law of the Catholic Church." —Albert Smith, Chancellor of the Archdiocese of Baltimore, replying for the Cardinal in a letter dated February 10, 1920.

If you observe Sunday, you observe a commandment of the Catholic Church. "It is well to remind the Presbyterians, Baptists, Methodists, and all other Christians, that the Bible does not support them anywhere in their observance of Sunday. Sunday is an institution of the Roman Catholic Church, and those who observe the day observe a commandment of the Catholic Church." —Priest Brady, in an address, reported in the Elizabeth, New Jersey *News,* March 18, 1903.

 **Sunday worship pays homage to the authority of the Catholic Church.** "It was the Catholic Church which, by the authority of JESUS CHRIST, has transferred this rest to the Sunday in remembrance of the resurrection of our Lord. Thus the observance of Sunday by the Protestants is an homage they pay, in spite of themselves, to the authority of the [Catholic] Church." —Monsignor Louis Gaston de Ségur ([1820–1881) French Catholic prelate, apologist, and diplomatic and judicial official at Rome), *Plain Talk about the Protestantism of To-day,* 1868, p. 225.

To observe Sunday is to accept the Pope's authority. "Protestants . . . accept Sunday rather than Saturday as the day for public worship after the Catholic Church made the change . . . But the Protestant mind does not seem to realize that in accepting the Bible, in observing the Sunday, they are accepting the authority of the spokesman for the church, the Pope." —*Our Sunday Visitor*, February 5, 1950.

Decrees of the Pope considered infallible. "All dogmatic decrees of the Pope, made with or without his general council, are infallible. . . . Once made, no pope or council can reverse them. . . . This is the Catholic principle, that the Church cannot err in faith." —*The Catholic World,* June 1871, pp. 422, 423.

Rome never changes. *"Let it be remembered, it is the boast of Rome that she never changes. The principles of Gregory VII and Innocent III are still the principles of the Roman Church."—The Great Controversy, p. 579.*

Gregory VII *(reigned 1073–1085)* was the Pope for whom King Henry IV waited barefoot in the snow to gain audience to receive forgiveness in January of 1077.

Pope Innocent III *(reigned 1198–1216)* excommunicated King John of England and put his kingdom under an interdict until John bowed to papal authority. He also called a very bloody crusade in 1208 against the Albigensians—Christian believers who desired to follow the Bible rather than Rome.

Not to question the Church. "We have no right to ask reasons of the church, any more than of Almighty God, as a preliminary to our submission. We are to take with unquestioning docility, whatever instruction the church gives us." —*The Catholic World*, August 1871, p. 589.

Catholic authority. "If a man refuse to hear the Church, let him be considered—so the Lord commands—as a heathen and a publican." —***Pope Pius XII***, in his encyclical letter, "The Mystical Body of Christ," June 29, 1943.

Inflated views of papal power. "We [the Pope] hold upon this earth the place of God Almighty." *—Pope Leo XIII*, Encyclical Letter "The Reunion of Christendom," dated June 20, 1894.

The pope ascribed authority to change divine law. "The pope can modify divine law, since his power is not of man, but of God, and he acts in the place of God upon earth, with the fullest power of binding and loosing his sheep." —Petrus de Ancharano quoted in Lucius Ferraris, *Prompta Bibliotheca,* vol. 6, 1772, p. 29, art. 2, "Papa."

"The Pope is not only the representative of Jesus Christ, but he is Jesus Christ Himself, hidden under veil of flesh." *—The Catholic National,* July, 1, 1895.

When the Pope speaks *ex cathedra*, his pronouncements are considered infallible. "The Roman Pontiff, when he speaks *ex cathedra*—that is, when in the exercise of his office as pastor and teacher of all Christians he defines, by virtue of his supreme Apostolic authority, a doctrine of faith or morals to be held by the whole Church—is . . . possessed of that infallibility with which the Divine Redeemer wished His Church to be endowed . . . and consequently that such definitions of the Roman Pontiff are irreformable of their own nature." *—The Catholic Encyclopedia,* 1910, vol. 7, p. 796.

Pope claims primacy over the whole world. "We define that the Holy Apostolic See and the Roman Pontiff hold the primacy over the whole world. . . ." —Council of Florence, Session XXV (July 6, 1439), Definitio, in Mansi, *Sacrorum Counciliorum,* vol. 31, col. 1031, Latin.

The Papacy sees itself as the foundation for a new geopolitical system. "Willing or not, ready or not, we are involved. . . . the competition is about who will establish the first one-world system of government that has ever existed in the society of nations. It is about who will hold and wield the dual power of authority and control over each of us as individuals and over all of us together as a community. . . .

"Our way of life as individuals and as citizens of the nations; our families and our jobs; our trade and commerce and money; our educational systems and our religions and our cultures; even the badges of our national identity, which most of us have always taken for granted—all will have been powerfully and radically altered forever. No one can be exempted from its effects. No sector of our lives will remain untouched." —Malachi Martin, *The Keys of This Blood,* 1990, p. 15.

The late Malachi Martin wrote as a former Jesuit and former professor of Vatican's Pontifical Biblical Institute.

"[John Paul II] insists that men have no reliable hope of creating a viable geopolitical system unless it is on the basis of Roman Catholic Christianity." —*Martin,* p. 492.

"In Papa Wojtyla's outlook, therefore, the Grand Design of which he is the nominated Servant is the design of divine providence to recall men to the values that derive only from belief, from religion and from divine revelation." —*Martin,* p. 656, 657.

Rome's ultimate triumph over her foes. "We believe in the triumph of the Catholic Church over infidelity, heresy, schism, revolution, and despotism; over Judaism, Mohammedanism, and heathenism. The restoration of the Pope's temporal kingdom is necessary to this triumph, and therefore we believe it will be restored." —*The Catholic World,* August 1877, p. 620.

The U.S. must also play a crucial role in the new world system. "The world, in fact, is undergoing a profound transformation. . . . Especially since the events of 1989 [the fall of Communism], the role of the United States in the world has taken on a new prominence. Your widespread influence is at once political, economic, military and, due to your communications, cultural." —Pope John Paul II, *Make Room for the Mystery of God,* pp. 7–9 (quoted in *Sunday's Coming,* p. 60).

"I say this too, to the United States to America: today, in our world as it is, many other nations and peoples look to you as the principal model and pattern for their own advancement in democracy." —Pope John Paul II, *Catholic News Service,* Oct. 9, 1995.

"I believe that the U.S., as the world's only superpower, and the Holy See ["the central government of the Roman Catholic Church," *Melady,* 178], as the only world-wide moral political sovereignty, have significant roles to play in the future. Their actions will impact the lives of people in all parts of the globe." —Thomas P. Melady U.S.-Vatican ambassador, 1989–1993, *The Ambassador's Story—The United States and the Vatican in World Affairs*, p. 10.

The more important issue. The importance of the seventh-day Sabbath for Christians becomes more apparent as we ask ourselves the question, "Which authority matters most to me?" If we answer that we are most concerned with what man thinks, then we should logically observe Sunday, for there could be no higher claim for human authority than to have set aside or altered a direct command of God. But, if we respond that it is the Bible that we most highly esteem, then we should observe the seventh-day Sabbath, for God's Word endorses no other day and teaches that nothing less than complete obedience to His commands will do. *Partial obedience is no obedience at all.* Numerous stories in the Bible emphasize God's displeasure with those who only partially obeyed His commands. He took the kingdom from King Saul when Saul claimed to have obeyed God's commandment, but had done so only in part (*1 Samuel 15:1–22*).

A fellow pastor once asked me, "Is the day all that important?"

I turned the question back to him and said,

"Is the authority of Scripture all that important?"

What authority matters most to you? How important is God's truth?

9

Should Christians minimize Bible truth for the sake of unity?

Recent meetings of religious leaders raise concerns about the accommodation of truth. "At his [the Pope's] invitation, leaders from the religions of the earth gathered . . . in the tranquil medieval Italian town of Assisi. . . . The assemblage included . . . believers in creeds once labeled 'heathen' and 'pagan' by a church that for centuries had preached unambiguously that there was no salvation outside its walls. The astonishing variety of the invited group also raised suspicions among some Christians that Assisi represented a heretical step toward syncretism, the amalgamation of various conflicting religions." —*Time,* November 10, 1986.

A new day for ecumenicism. "Heads of the American Protestant and Eastern Orthodox churches who were meeting with pope John Paul II on Friday hailed their first, broadly representative discussion as a landmark on the road to greater unity. . . . The Rev. Donald Jones, a United Methodist and chairman of the University of South Carolina religious studies department, termed it 'the most important ecumenical meeting of the century' . . . The Rev. Paul A. Crow, Jr., of Indianapolis, ecumenical officer of the Christian Church (Disciples of Christ), called it a 'new day in ecumenism' opening a future in which God 'is drawing us together.'" —*The Montgomery Advertiser,* September 12, 1987.

Past church opponents join hands as partners. "It was an unprecedented interlude, there in the overwhelmingly Protestant Southland Sept. 11, 1987, as Pope John Paul II led a Billy Graham-style service, using Graham's advisers, pulpit and sound equipment, in conjunction with the widest array of American church officials ever assembled with a pope. . . . 'The whole atmosphere has changed,' says religion historian Harry S. Stout of Yale University, noting that in television sermons it is generally impossible to tell a Catholic from a Protestant." —*The Courier,* Findlay, Ohio, March 29, 1988.

Baptist and Catholic theologians find common ground. Associated Press, NEW YORK—"Southern Baptists and Roman Catholics, the nation's two largest denominations, generally have been regarded as doctrinally far apart, but their scholars find they basically agree. . . . The 163-page report is seen as the most full-scale, mutual examination of respective positions of the two traditions. Achieving it was an unprecedented experience for Southern Baptists, commonly averse to ecumenical affairs. . . . The talks, sponsored by the Catholic Bishops' Committee on Ecumenical and Interreligious Affairs and the Southern Baptist Department of Interfaith Witness, involved 18 meetings between 1978 and 1988." —*The Bakersfield Californian,* August 27, 1989.

Anglican leader calls for unity under the Pope. Associated Press, ROME—"Anglican leader Archbishop called Saturday for all Christians to accept the Roman Catholic pope as a common leader 'presiding in love' 'for the universal church, I renew the plea,' he said. Could not all Christians come to reconsider the kind of primacy the bishop of Rome [the Pope] exercised within the early church?" —*The Dallas Morning News,* October 1, 1989.

Common issues between Protestants and Catholics. "Frankly, I feel I have a lot more in common with this pope than with liberal Protestants. The real battle is not between Protestants and Catholics anymore, it's between conservative Christians fighting for the fundamental truths of the faith, and liberals who deny the central truths of Christianity." —Pat Robertson, *Christian American,* October 1993.

Evangelicals and Roman Catholics agree not to proselytize. "An agreement was signed March 30, 1994, between Evangelicals and Roman Catholics, whereby they promised to stop proselytizing one another's members. This twenty-five page document, signed by thirty-nine leading Evangelical Protestants and Catholics, urges the country's 13 million Evangelicals and 52 million Catholics to work together toward world evangelism and societal concerns. However, this document represents the merging of two major religious groups that form the countries largest voting bloc. 'This is the wave of the future,' commented Reed. He described the new unity expressed in the agreement as evidence of a potential political coalition

Signers of Evangelicals and Catholics Together (from left) Catholic Richard John Neuhaus, head of the Institute on Religion and Public Life; Charles Colson, founder of Prison Fellowship; Catholic George Weigel, director of the Ethics and Policy Center; and Kent Hill, president of Eastern Nazarene College.

that will significantly influence American politics in the years to come." —Jeff Wehr, *Our Firm Foundation,* April 1996, p. 4.

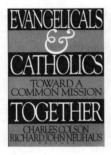

The "Evangelicals and Catholics Together" document acknowledges major differences between Evangelicals and Catholics. "We note some of the differences and disagreements that must be addressed more fully and candidly in order to strengthen between us a relationship of trust in obedience to truth. Among points of difference in doctrine, worship, practice, and piety that are frequently thought to divide us are these:

- The church as an integral part of the Gospel or the church as a communal consequence of the Gospel.
- The church as visible communion or invisible fellowship of true believers.
- The sole authority of Scripture (*sola scriptura*) or Scripture as authoritatively interpreted in the church.
- The soul freedom of the individual Christian or the Magisterium (teaching authority) of the community.
- The church as local congregation or universal communion.
- Ministry ordered in apostolic succession or the priesthood of all believers.
- Sacraments and ordinances as symbols of grace or means of grace.
- The Lord's Supper as eucharistic sacrifice or memorial meal.

- Remembrance of Mary and the saints or devotion to Mary and the saints.

- Baptism as sacrament of regeneration or testimony to regeneration.

".... On these questions, and other questions implied by them, Evangelicals hold that the Catholic Church has gone beyond Scripture, adding teachings and practices that detract from or compromise the Gospel of God's saving grace in Christ. Catholics, in turn, hold that such teachings and practices are grounded in Scripture and belong to the fullness of God's revelation. Their rejection, Catholics say, results in a truncated and reduced understanding of the Christian reality."—*Evangelicals and Catholics Together: The Christian Mission in the Third Millennium, signed March 29, 1994.*

Catholics still to confess their sins through the Church. "Pope John Paul II ... on Tuesday told Roman Catholics to seek forgiveness through the church and not directly from God. In a major document on the need for confession of sin, the pontiff laid down guidelines for the world's nearly 800 million Roman Catholics on the purpose of confessing sins to priests. .... The requirement for confessing sin through priests is one of the fundamental principles of Roman Catholicism." —*The Associated Press,* December 11, 1984.

The Pope encourages Marian devotion and use of indulgences. "Pope John Paul II's decision to set aside a special year devoted to Mary reflects his desire to bring back such traditional customs as pilgrimages to sanctuaries and religious possessions, Vatican officials say. ...

"The Vatican said the Catholics could gain indulgence, or the pardon of temporal punishment of sin, by devoutly taking part in some of the Marian year activities. ...

"From the outset of his pontificate more than eight years ago, John Paul has displayed special devotion to her. He calls Mary the 'heavenly mother of the church' and often invokes her intercession in public prayers." —*The Associated Press,* February 17, 1987.

But Jesus said: "I am the way, the truth, and the life: no man cometh unto the Father, but by me. . . . whatsoever ye shall ask in my name, that will I do, that the Father may be glorified in the Son." John 14:6, 13.

And Paul declared: "For there is one God, and one mediator between God and men, the man Christ Jesus." 1 Timothy 2:5.

The Pope declares that conscience should be subject to the Bible *and* Church tradition. "John Paul replies that true freedom must be united with moral truth, truth as reflected in a natural law that is evident to everyone and defined by the Bible and *Church tradition.* Otherwise, he says, each individual conscience becomes supreme—he even uses the word infallible. And in the clash of infallibilities, moral confusion reigns. Only absolute morality, argues the Pope, provides the basis for the democratic equality of all citizens, with common rights and duties and without 'privileges or exceptions.' In short, only when people hold to the same standards of good and evil can they be free and equal." —Richard N. Ostling, "A Refinement of Evil," *TIME,* October 4, 1993, *emphasis supplied.*

Lutherans and Catholics sign joint statement. "On Oct. 31, 1999, for the first time in 487 years, the Catholic and Lutheran churches signed a joint doctrinal statement, the 'Joint Declaration on the Doctrine of Justification.'

"The signing took place in Augsburg, Germany, where in 1530, the Augsburg Confession—the founding document of the Lutheran Church—was drafted. The document was signed by delegations

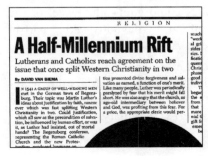

from the Vatican and the Lutheran World Federation (LWF), a global communion of Lutheran churches, including the evangelical Lutheran Church in America." —Erin Piroutek, *The Observer,* University Wire, South Bend, Indiana, November 1, 1999.

70

But Rome acknowledges only one true religion. "Nowhere is dogmatic intolerance so necessary a rule of life as in the domain of religious belief, since for each individual his eternal salvation is at stake. Just as there can be no alternative multiplication tables, so there can be but a single true religion, which, by the very fact of its existence, protests against all other religions as false." —*The Catholic Encyclopedia, 1911 edition,* vol. 14, p. 765.

Pope says only Rome has the fullness of the means of salvation. "Pope John Paul II urged 'all Christians' to mobilize for evangelism and to prepare for what he believes will be 'the dawning of a new missionary age.' . . . The pope stated at one point in his message that the mission of world evangelism must be conducted with the conviction that the Catholic Church 'alone possesses the fullness of the means of salvation.'" —*National & International Religion Report,* Feb. 11, 1991.

Protestants to return to Rome. "They [Protestants] conveniently forget that they separated from us, not we from them; and that it is for them to return to unity on Catholic terms, not for us to seek union with them, or to accept it, on their terms. . . . Protestantism is rebellion against the authority of Christ vested in His Church. . . ." —*America* [Catholic periodical], January 4, 1941, vol. 64, p. 343.

A call to return to the Mother Church. "It's time for Protestants to go to the shepherd [the Pope] and say 'what do we have to do to come home?'" —*Dr. Robert Schuller, Los Angeles Herald Examiner,* September 19, 1987.

Roman Catholicism increasing in favor with Protestants. "Romanism is now regarded by Protestants with far greater favor than in former years. . . The time was when Protestants placed a high value upon the liberty of conscience which had been so dearly purchased. They taught their children to abhor popery and held that to seek harmony with Rome would be disloyalty to God. But how widely different are the sentiments now expressed!" —Ellen G. White, *The Great Controversy,* p. 563.

Have we not all seen just how quickly attitudes in our country can change? *Would it take that much of an imagination to picture, with the current ecumenical climate, for a few more catastrophic events to jolt religious Americans into pressing for laws to "encourage" people to set aside special time for church and family?* There are those who are already in favor of such legislation.

10

A new impetus for Sunday legislation

Sanctification of Sunday is a part of Rome's overall plan. "VATICAN CITY, Sept. 8.—Pope Pius XII told a throng of 250,000 Catholic worshippers gathered in St. Peter's Square yesterday that 'the time for reflection and planning is past,' in religious and moral fields, and the 'time for action' has arrived. . . . The Pope . . . declared that the battle in religious and moral fields hinged on five points: Religious culture, the sanctifying of Sunday, the savings [*sic*] of the Christian family, social justice and loyalty and truthfulness in dealings." —Associated Press, "Pope Calls for Moral and Religious Action, Not Just Planning" *Evening Star* (Washington, D.C.), Sept. 8, 1947, p. A-12.

Christians are encouraged to seek civil recognition of Sunday. "In respecting religious liberty and the common good of all, Christians should seek recognition of Sundays and the Church's holy days as legal holidays."—*Catechism of the Catholic Church,* 1994, p. 585.

The Pope's intentions for the world can be seen in his call for mandatory Sunday closing laws in Europe. "The blue law issue is expected to be contentious throughout Europe as the European Economic Community struggles to determine policy for member nations. John Paul II continues to press for mandatory Sunday-closing laws in all EEC nations. Recently the pope called for nations to resist trends to regard Sunday as a work day. Blue laws, the pope said, help protect 'the precious time for liturgical life and spiritual renewal.'" —*Church & State,* May, 1992, p. 19.

European Community forcing Sundays off. "God said everyone should have a day off a week. Muslims chose Fridays, Jews Saturdays, Christians Sundays. Now the European Community is pretending to be God. It is about to decree that EC citizens must take Sundays off." —*Economist,* October 19, 1991, p. 16.

Pope appeals for civil Sunday legislation in *Dies Domini.* "Therefore, also in the particular circumstances of our own time, Christians will naturally strive to ensure that civil legislation respects their duty to keep Sunday holy. In any case, they are obliged in conscience to arrange their Sunday rest in a way which allows them to take part in the Eucharist, refraining from work and activities which are incompatible with the sanctification of the Lord's Day, with its characteristic joy and necessary rest for spirit and body." —Pope John Paul II, May 31, 1998, *Dies Domini.*

Apparition of Mary calls for Sunday preservation. "One evening Our Lady appeared to a local farmer, Michael O'Donnell. She told him, 'preserve Sunday for prayer'" —Ted and Maureen Flynn, *The Thunder of Justice,* p. 30.

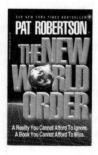 **Pat Robertson laments nullifying of Sunday laws.** "There will never be world peace until God's house and God's people are given their rightful place of leadership at the top of the world. . . . Laws in America that mandated a day of rest [i.e., Sunday "blue laws"] from incessant commerce have been nullified as a violation of the separation of church and state." —Pat Robertson, *The New World Order,* pp. 227, 236.

Appeal for Americans to ask for Sunday laws. "All Americans would do well to petition the president and the congress to make a federal law—an amendment to the constitution if need be—to establish the Sabbath as a national day of rest so that religious and non-religious Americans can rest in peace." —John Lanaro, *Catholic Twin Circle,* August 25, 1985, quoted in *Church and State Magazine,* October 1985.

Sunday laws and Catholic authority. "Strange as it may seem, the State, in passing laws for the due sanctification of Sunday, is unwittingly acknowledging the authority of the Catholic Church, and carrying out more or less faithfully its prescriptions." —John Gilmary Shea, "The Observance of Sunday and Civil Laws for Its Enforcement," *The American Catholic Quarterly Review,* 8 (January, 1883), p. 139.

The divine call for worship

Thus the heavens and the earth were finished, and all the host of them. [2] And on the seventh day God ended his work which he had made; and he rested on the seventh day from all his work which he had made. [3] And God blessed the seventh day, and sanctified it: because that in it he had rested from all his work which God created and made. —Genesis 2:1–3.

Remember the Sabbath day, to keep it holy. [9] Six days shalt thou labour, and do all thy work: [10] But the seventh day is the Sabbath of the LORD thy God: in it thou shalt not do any work, thou, nor thy son, nor thy daughter, thy manservant, nor thy maidservant, nor thy cattle, nor thy stranger that is within thy gates: [11] For in six days the LORD made heaven and earth, the sea, and all that in them is, and rested the seventh day: wherefore the LORD blessed the Sabbath day, and hallowed it. —Exodus 20:8–11.

And he came to Nazareth, where he had been brought up: and, as his custom was, he went into the synagogue on the Sabbath day, and stood up for to read. —Luke 4:16.

And he said unto them, The Sabbath was made for man, and not man for the Sabbath: [28] Therefore the Son of man is Lord also of the Sabbath. —Mark 2:27, 28.

There remaineth therefore a rest [Gr. "a Sabbath keeping"] to the people of God. . . . Not forsaking the assembling of ourselves together, as the manner of some is; . . . —Hebrews 4:9; 10:25.

Thou art worthy, O Lord, to receive glory and honour and power: for thou hast created all things, and for thy pleasure they are and were created. —Revelation 4:11.

And the dragon was wroth with the woman, and went to make war with the remnant of her seed, which keep the commandments of God, and have the testimony of Jesus Christ. —Revelation 12:17.

And I saw another angel fly in the midst of heaven, having the everlasting gospel to preach unto them that dwell on the earth, and to every nation, and kindred, and tongue, and people, [7] Saying with a loud voice, Fear God, and give glory to him; for the hour of his judgment is come: and worship him that made heaven, and earth, and the sea, and the fountains of waters. . . . Here is the patience of the saints: here are they that keep the commandments of God and the faith of Jesus. —Revelation 14:6, 7, 12.

11

What does the evidence say to you?

*T*he Bible reveals that, from the beginning, there has been but one day upon which the Creator rested and which He blessed, set apart, and commanded to be kept as the "Sabbath of the Lord thy God" (*Genesis 2:1–3; Exodus 20:10; Revelation 14:6, 7)*. The Bible also reveals:

➤ that, on this same day, Jesus *and* His Apostles met with others for worship (*Luke 4:16; Acts 17:2*)

➤ that, before the end, "the saints" will be set apart by their keeping of the commandments (*Revelation 12:17; 14:12),* and

➤ that, in the earth made new, the Sabbath will be observed by all people (*Isaiah 66:22, 23)*.

By contrast, *history* reveals that popular Christianity took a detour from the path of revealed Bible truth—traveling a twisting trail of human philosophy, pagan practice, and ecclesiastical tradition (*Mark 7:13; 2 Thessalonians 2:3; Colossians 2:8),* establishing a day that God never sanctified.

In light of this evidence, how will you respond?

"So what"?

"Yeh, but . . ."?

Or, *"Now what"?*

I hope that, by now, you've moved beyond the indifference of *"so what"* and been satisfied by the biblical and historical answers to the *"yeh, but,"* so that you are ready and willing to utter the words, *"Now what?"* —"Now what do you want me to do, Lord?"

Dear reader, if you accept the Bible as a guide for your life and you truly want to worship the Creator in spirit and in truth, why wouldn't you want to experience the blessing that He has placed upon the day that He set aside for rest and worship?

12

Questions about the Sabbath answered

*M*ore and more Christians—the world over—are
discovering the beauty and practicality of God's holy
Sabbath and are convinced that it should be a part of their
lives. According to *The Directory of Sabbath-Observing Groups,*
ninth edition, there are now over 400 Sabbatarian denominations and
groups, including over 1600 congregations in the United States of
America alone.

Yet, for some, certain questions about the Sabbath and the New
Testament remain. The most common of these are here answered.

Q₁ **In the gospels, Jesus doesn't seem to say much about the
Sabbath except to object to all its restrictions (*Matthew
12*). Doesn't He teach that the Sabbath was instituted
primarily for man's *physical* needs (*Mark 2:27*)?**

It is a matter of scriptural record that, by the man-made restrictions
which they imposed upon the Sabbath, *the Jewish teachers* made the
Sabbath into something God never intended—a burdensome experience (*Matthew 12; John 5*). But Jesus' efforts to remove the human
requirements from the Sabbath should not be taken as an indication
that He wanted to do away with the *spiritual* dimension of the
Sabbath—the day which He Himself had made and *blessed* for the
welfare of mankind. (The Sabbath was made for man, *Mark 2:27;*
Jesus made all things, *John 1:3; Colossians 1:16; Hebrews 1:2;* therefore, it was Jesus who made the Sabbath, *Mark 2:28.*) Jesus worked to
free the commandments of the artificial, man-made additions that
covered up their original beauty and purpose (*Isaiah 42:21*).

The *fourth* commandment was not the only commandment that
was obscured by the teachings of the Jewish teachers. The *fifth*
commandment was also obscured by a tradition of the Pharisees
known as "Corban" (which allowed them to avoid supporting their

elderly parents by "dedicating" their money as a gift to the temple, while using the money for themselves.) It was because of this tradition that Jesus said:

"Howbeit in vain do they worship me, teaching for doctrines the commandments of men. . . . Making the word of God of none effect through your tradition . . ." Mark 7:7–13.

Addressing the abuse of a commandment is very different from invalidating the commandment itself. Jesus' fresh, spiritual approach to God's commandments was not with the intent of abolishing or lowering the standard of human responsibility, but was to lead the human family into a deeper understanding of God's ideal for His children. (See *Matthew 5:22, 28* on murder and adultery and *Matthew 15:3–9* on honoring our parents.)

The truth is, Jesus *did* teach about the Sabbath. How was that? By both *precept* and *example.* (As the following text illustrates, a spoken precept is not the only way to teach something.)

"And they were all amazed, insomuch that they questioned among themselves, saying, What thing is this? what <u>new doctrine</u> is this? for with authority commandeth he even the unclean spirits, and they do obey him." Mark 1:27.

Jesus didn't teach this "new doctrine" (regarding the casting out of unclean spirits) by a spoken precept, but by His living *example* (which was His method of choice in teaching about the Sabbath).

Through the many instances of Jesus' activities on the Sabbath, He taught the "new doctrine" that the Sabbath is not only for *rest* and *worship,* but for *uplifting social interaction* and *ministry* to those in need. (*Nine instances* in *Matthew, 12:1, 2, 5, 8, 10, 11, 12; 24:20; 28:1;* **ten** in *Mark, 1:21; 2:23, 24, 27, 28; 3:2, 4; 6:2; 15:42; 16:1;* **seventeen** in *Luke, 4:16, 31; 6:1, 2, 5, 6, 7, 9; 13:10, 14, 15, 16; 14:1, 3, 5; 23:54, 56;* and **nine** in *John, 5:9, 10, 16, 18; 7:22, 23; 9:14, 16; 19:31.*)

In addition to these many instances of Jesus' example, He taught—by precept—that the Sabbath was "made" for man's benefit. Later—by precept—He admonished His disciples to pray that they not have to flee from Jerusalem on the Sabbath (*Matthew 24:20)* when it would be surrounded by Roman armies (*Matthew 24:15; Mark 13:14; Luke 21:20).*

Why did Jesus instruct them to pray this prayer? Was it merely a practical matter, arising from His concern that His followers not be trapped in Jerusalem by Jewish prohibitions concerning Sabbath travel, or was He not also looking out for their spiritual benefit as He had been when He instructed them to "*pray* that" they "enter not into temptation" (*Luke 22:40)*? We know from history that the believers who fled Judea, known as "Nazarenes" (*Acts 24:5)*, were still observing the Sabbath at the time they escaped to Pella in 66 A.D. Likewise, their descendants continued to do so even down to the time when the Christian historian, Epiphanius (*Panarion* 29) was writing in the fourth century. Jesus knew—some 35 years before the events—what impact His words would have on His disciples, for, in praying that special prayer, they could never forget their Lord's special day.

Q₂ **Why should we observe the Sabbath when Jesus didn't specifically tell us to keep it?**

The argument of silence—what Jesus didn't tell us—actually speaks more eloquently in favor of worshipping on the Sabbath than not, for we have no record that Jesus ever told His disciples to *stop* worshipping on the Sabbath or that He ever told them to *start* worshipping on Sunday (notwithstanding what the Church that claimed to be His representatives decided to do years later).

We often hear people say that the Sabbath commandment is the only commandment of the Ten not reinstated in the Christian era because—they assume—it is the only one not quoted in the New Testament. But there is a major flaw in this line of reasoning, for, even though the last six commandments are quoted several times in the New Testament, *none of the first four commandments ever are.*

Of the last six, the **fifth** commandment is quoted in *Matthew 15:4; Mark 7:10; Ephesians 6:2*, the **sixth** in *Matthew 5:21* and *James 2:11*, the **seventh** in *Matthew 5:27* and *James 2:11*, and the **tenth** in *Romans 7:7*. Then, in *Romans 13:9*, Paul quotes the **sixth** through the **tenth**, and Jesus quotes the **fifth** through the **ninth** in *Matthew 19:18–19; Mark 10:19;* and *Luke 18:20*. But none of the first four commandments are ever directly quoted. If the New Testament's failure to quote a commandment means release from the obligation to observe it, then Christians are now free (1) to have other gods before Jehovah, (2) to worship idols, (3) to take God's name in vain, and (4) to forget His Sabbath. But is there anyone who would want to champion such a view?

Digging a little deeper in the New Testament, we find ample support for the first four commandments. Jesus upholds the **first** commandment when He quotes *Deuteronomy 6:13, 14* in *Matthew 4:10*. Paul upholds the **second** in *Acts 17:29* and *1 Corinthians 8:6*. Both Jesus and James support the **third** commandment (with regard to taking false oaths and controlling our words) in *Matthew 5:33–37* and *James 1:26*. And both Jesus and Paul support the **fourth** commandment by their regular observance of the Sabbath (*Luke 4:16; Acts 17:2*), while *Hebrews* declares that, as God rested in the creation, there still remains a Sabbath rest for the people of God (*Hebrews 4:4, 9*), and *Revelation,* in language closely resembling that of the fourth commandment, foretells that God's faithful people in the end times will worship Him as Creator, keeping His commandments.

> ". . . *worship him that made heaven, and earth, and the sea, and the fountains of waters . . . Here is the patience of the saints: here are they that keep the commandments of God, and the faith of Jesus.*" —*Revelation 14:7, 12.*

Q₃ The Jews kept the Sabbath as a memorial of creation, but shouldn't we Christians keep Sunday in memorial of the Resurrection?

Though the Jews were indeed entrusted with God's memorial of the Creation, the Sabbath was not made for the Jews alone, but for all of mankind.

> ". . . The Sabbath was established originally in no special connection with the Hebrews, but as an institution for all mankind, in commemoration of God's rest after the six days of creation. It was designed for all the descendants of Adam." —Adult *Quarterly,* Southern Baptist Convention series, Aug. 15, 1937.

If the first Sabbath to be kept by a human being were just before Sinai (*Exodus 16*), and the Sabbath were merely a Jewish institution, as some claim, then why did Jesus say that the Sabbath was "made for *man*"? And, if no one was keeping the Sabbath, how then did generation after generation of human beings keep track of the weekly cycle for all those years? It is obvious from the book of Genesis, that the patriarchs used the seven-day week to count time *(Genesis 2:1–3; 7:4, 10; 8:10, 12; 29:27, 28; 31:23; 50:10)*. Furthermore, the seventh day held special significance in many ancient cultures outside of Judaism. Take the ancient Babylonians and Greeks, for example:

> "The Sabbath-rest was a Babylonian, as well as a Hebrew, institution. . . . The Sabbath was also known, at all events in Accadian times, as a 'dies nefastus,' a day on which certain work was forbidden to be done, and an old list of Babylonian festivals and fast-days tells us that on the seventh, fourteenth, nineteenth, twenty-first, and twenty-eighth days each month the Sabbath-rest had to be observed." —A. H. Sayce, *The Higher Criticism and the Monuments,* 1895, p. 74.

> "But the seventh day is recognized as sacred, not by the Hebrews only, but also by the Greeks." —Clement of Alexandria.

One would also wonder how the story of the creation would have been maintained from generation to generation—a story which places special significance on the seventh day—if no one had ever observed the Sabbath during the 2500 years between creation and Sinai. The creation story itself testifies that the Sabbath belongs to all people:

> "But after the whole world had been completed according to the perfect nature of the number six, the Father hallowed the day following, the seventh, praising it, and calling it holy. For that day is the festival, not of one city or one country, but of all the earth; a day which alone it is right to call the day of festival for all people, and the birthday of the world." —Philo, "On the Creation," XXX (89).

So, although the Scriptures do clearly portray the Sabbath as being the memorial of God's creation rest *(Genesis 2:1–3; Exodus 20:11; Hebrews 4:4)* and the early hours of the first day as the time when Christ arose from the dead *(Matthew 28:1)*, nowhere do they identify Sunday worship as a commemoration of the resurrection (or as a replacement for Sabbath observance). Instead, they identify partaking of the *Eucharist* (or *communion service)* as the commemoration of "the Lord's death" and the participation of the believer in *baptism* as the symbol of the Lord's death and resurrection.

"For as often as ye eat this bread, and drink this cup, ye do shew the Lord's death till he come." 1 Corinthians 11:26.

"Therefore we are buried with him by baptism into death: that like as Christ was raised up from the dead by the glory of the Father, even so we also should walk in newness of life. ⁵ For if we have been planted together in the likeness of his death, we shall be also in the likeness of his resurrection." Romans 6:4, 5.

Q₄ **Since so many important events following Jesus' crucifixion occurred on the first day of the week, doesn't that make Sunday the biblical "Lord's Day" instead of Saturday?**

While important events did occur on the first day of the week, the New Testament writers themselves, in telling the story years after it occurred, consistently describe the day of the resurrection as the "third day" *(Acts 10:40; 1 Corinthians 15:4)* and never draw the conclusion that these biblical events made Sunday the "Lord's Day." It would take the Church another hundred years from the time of the resurrection to make such a claim. (The first statements which base Sunday observance—at least in part—on the resurrection were written by pseudo-Barnabas and Justin Martyr around 130 A.D.)

The New Testament writers do boldly declare that Christ rose on the "first of the week" *(Matthew 28:1; Mark 16:2, 9; Luke 24:1, 7, 21, 46; John 20:1),* yet only after they specifically note the passing of the Sabbath and its observance "according to the commandment," *(Matthew 28:1; Mark 16:1; Luke 24:56).* They describe how, following the Sabbath rest, Jesus met again and again that first day with His disciples to turn their fear and despair into faith and hope—appearing to Mary *(Mark 16:9),* to the disciples on the road to Emmaus *(Mark 16:12; Luke 24:13-33),* to Simon *(Luke 24:34),* and to *ten* of Jesus' disciples, who were gathered in the upper room, not for worship, but "for fear of the Jews" *(John 20:19).* They tell us that Jesus appeared "eight days" later (presumably the first day of the week, though neither Mark nor John make a point of this), to show

Himself to be the risen Savior, when Thomas had assembled at last with the other ten disciples in the upper room (*Mark 16:14; John 20:26-28*). Last of all, the book of *Acts* describes the outpouring of the Holy Spirit on the day of Pentecost (another Sunday since it came 50 days after the first day of the "Feast of Unleavened Bread"). But none of the New Testament writers ever tell us that Christ called for His followers to worship Him on any other day besides the Sabbath. *If these writers wanted us to see these events as inaugurating Sunday as the new day of Christian worship, why didn't they just say so?*

The fact that Christians of many countries continued worshipping on Sabbath for many years after the resurrection and that it took so long for Christians to begin meeting on Sunday (and did not cite the Apostles as support for the practice) shows that the disciples saw nothing about the Sunday resurrection that would nullify or replace the biblical seventh-day Sabbath—the only day over which God the Father and Son have claimed lordship (*Exodus 20:10; Mark 2:28*) and which can *biblically* be called the "Lord's Day."

Q₅ Didn't Paul observe the Sabbath in *Acts* only to make it easier for him to reach the Jews?

The Sabbath is mentioned a total of **nine times** in the book of *Acts* (*1:12; 13:14, 27, 42, 44; 15:21; 16:13; 17:2; 18:4*). In nearly every passage, the focus is on ministry to the Gentiles, as well as to the Jews. After all, Paul was "the Apostle to the Gentiles" (*Romans 11:13*).

In *Acts 13:42*, the Gentiles specifically asked for Paul to preach to them the following Sabbath.

"And when the Jews were gone out of the synagogue, the Gentiles besought that these words might be preached to them the next Sabbath."

If Paul were meeting on Sunday in somebody's house or school (as he actually did do "daily" in *Acts 19:9*), he missed a golden opportunity to advertise his Sunday morning meetings. *But there were no Sunday morning meetings to advertise. There was no "alternative" Sunday morning service!* That's why the whole city came back to hear him the next Sabbath *(13:44)*, which is just the first example of how the book of *Acts* takes for granted that Jews and Gentiles would be meeting for study and worship on the Sabbath.

Although *Acts 14:1*, strictly speaking, does not mention the Sabbath, still it establishes that, when Paul spoke in the synagogue of Iconium (which was undoubtedly on the Sabbath), both Jews and Greeks (Gentiles) were present and believed.

In *Acts 15:21*, James states that the requirements of the council for the Gentiles have already been taught every Sabbath in the various synagogues. In other words, at the time of the counsel in Jerusalem, James took for granted that Gentiles were attending worship services on the Sabbath.

"For Moses of old time hath in every city them that preach him, being read in the synagogues every Sabbath day." Acts 15:21.

Even *Acts 16:13* connects the Gentiles with the Sabbath, since the reason that the group was meeting beside the river was presumably because there were not enough Jewish men in town to form a synagogue. Lydia, the leader of the group, is described as a woman who "worshipped God." Now, if Lydia were a Jew, why would Luke use these words in describing her? What would be so distinctive about a Jew who worshipped God? It makes more sense to see her as a "god-fearing" Gentile who was leading out in a ladies' prayer group which met on the Sabbath.

That this lady was a "God-fearing" Gentile makes even more sense as we read about the "devout Greeks" in Thessalonica *(Acts 17:4)*, who believed in Jesus as a result of Paul's reasoning with them "three Sabbath days," and about the Jews and Greeks whom Paul persuaded *(Acts 18:4)* "every Sabbath" while he was in Corinth.

Taken in its entirety, the evidence confirms what Hugh Smith has written: the early Jewish and Gentile believers *both* worshipped on the Sabbath. And Paul used this common time of worship for evangelism.

Q₆ **Didn't the apostles worship on the first day of the week *(Acts 20:7)*? And didn't Paul command the Corinthians to**

bring their offering to Church on Sunday (*1 Corinthians 16:2*)? And didn't God honor Sunday by giving John the Revelation on that day *(Revelation 1:10)?*

What *do* these verses tell us about early church practice?

Acts 20:7. This passage describes a unique meeting for Paul. Since he was "ready to depart on the morrow;" he "continued his speech" on "Saturday night" *(New English Bible)* "until midnight." This late-night meeting hardly represents a pattern of church attendance for either Paul or the early church. His regular pattern or "custom" *(Acts 17:2)* is delineated throughout *chapters 13, 16, 17, and 18.* Honestly, does it really make sense to think that Paul would suddenly break his established pattern of Sabbath observance—without warning or explanation—and start observing Sunday in chapter 20?

1 Corinthians 16:2. This verse is not a command for the Corinthian believers to bring an offering to meeting on Sunday, but counsel that each believer should "lay by him in store" on the first of each week. Weymouth's version spells out more clearly the instructions for each Corinthian believer. Each was to "put on one side and store up *at his home* whatever gain has been granted to him" *(emphasis supplied).* While Malachi 3:10 does speak of a "storehouse" for the tithe (which, in our time, is often used to signify the church treasury), the church "storehouse" is not what this passage is describing. It does not say that the Corinthians were to bring their money to the storehouse, but that each was to individually "lay by him in store." This is a practice that it would be well for us to emulate, for we too should put aside money for God's work on a systematic or budgeted basis rather than only digging into our pockets at the spur of the moment when a need is presented or an offering plate is passed.

Revelation 1:10. In this verse, John does use the phrase "the Lord's day" to describe the Lord's appearance to him, but he does not identify which day that was. If we go outside the Bible, we will eventually find "Church Fathers" who use this phrase to refer to Sunday, but . . .

"There is no direct Scriptural authority for designating the first day 'the Lord's Day.'"—Dr. D. H. Lucas (*Disciples of Christ*), *The Christian Oracle,* January 23, 1890.

And, if we ask *the Scriptures alone* to answer the question of which is the "Lord's day," we will consistently find that, even though every day belongs to God ("This is the day which the Lord hath made; we will rejoice and be glad in it." *Psalm 118:24*), there is but one day that He claims as His special day. That day is the seventh-day Sabbath, "the rest of the holy Sabbath unto the LORD" (*Exodus 16:23*), "the Sabbath of the Lord thy God" (*Exodus 20:10; Leviticus 23:3; Deuteronomy 5:14)*—the day that God calls "My holy day" (*Isaiah 58:13*) and the only day over which Jesus specifically claims lordship (*Matthew 12:8; Mark 2:28;* and *Luke 6:5*).

Q₇ Like circumcision, isn't the Sabbath an obsolete Old Testament law that doesn't apply to Christians (*Romans 14:5, 6*)?

It is true that circumcision and the Sabbath were both laws in the Old Testament, but there are some substantial differences between the two institutions. First, while circumcision was instituted during the time of Abraham, the Sabbath goes back to the creation of mankind. Second, it was not the Sabbath that was singled out by Paul as a violation of Christian liberty, but rather circumcision. Those of "the circumcision party" insisted that adult male Gentiles be subjected to the major surgery of circumcision before they could become believers in Christ. But Paul argued that it was not essential that a person be circumcised in order for him to become a part of "the Israel of God" (*Galatians 6:16; Romans 2:28, 29)* or for him to "keep the righteousness of the law" (*Romans 2:25, 26*).

"For circumcision verily profiteth, if thou keep the law: but if thou be a breaker of the law, thy circumcision is made uncircumcision. ²⁶Therefore if the uncircumcision keep the righteousness of the law, shall not his uncircumcision be counted for circumcision?" Romans 2:25–26.

In three parallel statements, Paul contrasts that which is essential with that which is not.

"For in Christ Jesus neither circumcision availeth any thing, nor uncircumcision, but a new creature." Galatians 6:15.

"For in Jesus Christ neither circumcision availeth any thing, nor uncircumcision; but faith which worketh by love." Galatians 5:6.

"Circumcision is nothing, and uncircumcision is nothing, but the keeping of the commandments of God." 1 Corinthians 7:19.

The beloved Apostle John, who defines sin in terms of transgression of the law (*1 John 3:4*), also tells us how those who are born again through faith demonstrate their love for God:

"By this we know that we love the children of God, when we love God, and keep his commandments.[3] For this is the love of God, that we keep his commandments: and his commandments are not grievous." 1 John 5:2–3.

The "new covenant" does not do away with God's laws, but writes them in our hearts.

"For this is the covenant that I will make with the house of Israel after those days, saith the Lord; I will put my laws into their mind, and write them in their hearts: and I will be to them a God, and they shall be to me a people." Hebrews 8:10.

When we are "in Christ" and the law is within our hearts, we do not need to force ourselves to do what is right, for we serve God from the heart, by the power of the Holy Spirit, as Jesus and Paul taught:

"God is a Spirit: and they that worship him must worship him in spirit and in truth." John 4:24.

"But now we are delivered from the law, that being dead wherein we were held; that we should serve in newness of spirit, and not in the oldness of the letter." Romans 7:6.

When we submit our wills to Him and He comes into our hearts, He brings obedience to His Father's commandments with Him and we find freedom in living out His love. We find liberty in keeping His law.

"If ye keep my commandments, ye shall abide in my love; even as I have kept my Father's commandments, and abide in his love." John 15:10.

> *"To them that are without law, as without law, (being not without law to God, but <u>under the law to Christ</u>,) that I might gain them that are without law." 1 Corinthians 9:21.*

> *"If ye fulfill the <u>royal law</u> according to the scripture, Thou shalt love thy neighbour as thyself, ye do well: ⁹ But if ye have respect to persons, ye commit sin, and are convinced of the law as transgressors.¹⁰ For whosoever shall keep the whole law, and yet offend in one point, he is guilty of all.¹¹ For he that said, Do not commit adultery, said also, Do not kill. Now if thou commit no adultery, yet if thou kill, thou art become a transgressor of the law.¹² So speak ye, and so do, as they that shall be judged by the <u>law of liberty</u>." James 2:8–12.*

And what about **Romans 14:5, 6?** As tempting as it might be to read into this passage a discussion of whether or not Christians are obligated to keep the Sabbath, the statement does *not* say: "One man esteems one day and another man esteems another." It says: "*One man esteemeth one day above another: another esteemeth every day alike.*" In verse 6, the "esteeming" of a particular day is connected with eating or not eating. Thus the topic of discussion was days for voluntary fasting and not days for worship (which had not yet become an issue at this point in church history).

The *Didache* (8:1) attests that particular days for fasting were at issue in the early church. The document warns Christians not to fast with the hypocrites on the *second* and *fifth* days of the week, but on the *fourth* day and *sixth* day (literally *paraskeuēn* or "preparation"). Incidentally, in using the name "the preparation" for the sixth day of the week (Friday being the day when Sabbath keepers "prepare" for the Sabbath), the *Didache* provides indirect evidence that, some time during the document's compilation, Christian believers were keeping the Sabbath.

Q₈ **Doesn't the New Testament teach that the main thing is to love our neighbor as ourselves (*Romans 13:9; Galatians 5:14*) and not to be so picky about every commandment? How could the Sabbath still be important to Christians if it is only mentioned two times outside the Gospels and the book of Acts (*Hebrews 4:4 and Colossians 2:16*)?**

Of course, the *main* thing is not the *only* thing. Even though the New Testament doesn't present Sabbath keeping as its *most* important theme, neither does it single it out for the "recycle bin." From start to finish, the New Testament never countenances commandment breaking. *John 14:15* does not say, If you love me, keep *most of* my commandments. Neither does *1 John 5:2, 3* say, By this we know that we love the children of God, when we love God and—*generally speaking*—keep his commandments, or For this is the love of God, that we keep *the majority of* his commandments: and his commandments are not grievous (*except for maybe one*). Love for our neighbor and love for God should not be used as an excuse for disobedience to any of God's requirements. Surrendered to the Holy Spirit, we keep God's commandments and bring joy to His heart, while enraging the devil, who sees that his time is running out and we still persist in trusting God and obeying Him (*Revelation 12:12, 17*).

Setting aside, for a moment, the lengthy list of Sabbath texts in the Gospels and Acts (which were compiled many years after the events they describe took place, without any comment about a change in the Sabbath), let us consider the verses in *Hebrews* and *Colossians*.

Hebrews' testimony adds a significant dimension to our understanding of the Sabbath. **Hebrews 4:4** begins by establishing that God rested on the seventh day. Then, just a few verses later (*4:9, 10*), it reminds us—in the context of resting from our own works—that there continues to be a *Sabbath* "rest" for the people of God. The Greek word for "rest" in this verse, *sabbatismos,* is unique. It is not the same Greek word for "rest," *katapausis,* used in *3:11, 18; 4:1, 3, 4, 5, 8, 10,* and *11*. Its meaning is different. While *katapausis* means "a calming" or "a resting place," *sabbatismos* is defined by *Bauer, Arndt, & Gingrich* as "Sabbath rest, Sabbath observance." *Brown, Driver, Briggs* says that it is derived from the noun *sabbaton* ("Sabbath"), while *Vine's* and *Moulton's* say that it is related to the verb *sabbatizo* (used several times in the Greek *Septuagint* version of the Old Testament: *Exodus 16:30; Leviticus 23:32; 26:34; 2 Chronicles 36:21*). According to *Bauer, Arndt, & Gingrich*, the verb means: "keep the Sabbath." Hence, a literal translation of *Hebrews 4:9* would be: "So then there remains a Sabbath observance to the people of God." For all that this passage does say, there is one thing that it clearly does *not* say—that the seventh-day Sabbath has been abolished!

"The fact that the author is not engaged in a polemic defense of the validity of Sabbath observance, but rather in an exhortation to experience its blessing which 'remains . . . for the people of God' (4:9), makes his testimony all the more valuable, since it takes its observance for granted. . . ." —Samuele Bacchiocchi, *From Sabbath to Sunday,* p. 65.

And what about *Colossians 2:14–17?* Does the nailing of the "handwriting of ordinances" (or hand-written legal document) to the cross indicate that the Sabbath has been abolished?

Although Paul declares in *Romans 3:31* that faith does not "make void the law," in *Ephesians 2:15,* he says that there is a "law of commandments contained in ordinances" that has been made void. (The terms "abolish" of *Ephesians 2:15* and "make void" of *Romans 3:31* are the same word in Greek, *katargeō*.) Is this a contradiction? No, the law of ordinances that was abolished is the *ceremonial (or sacrificial)* law and not the *moral* law of Ten Commandments. The *handwritten* "book of Moses," containing the sacrificial law, was placed *beside* the ark that contained the Ten Commandments. It stood as a testimony "against" the Jews (*2 Chronicles 35:12; Deuteronomy 31:26)* and, with its later Jewish embellishments, was "contrary" (literally, "an adversary") to both Jew and Gentile, forming an inseparable wall between the two (*Ephesians 2:14).* It was these embellishments of the law—the multitudinous doctrines and traditions of the rabbis—that Jesus condemned as "commandments of men" (*Matthew 5:3, 6; 15:9)* and that Peter called a "vain manner of life handed down from your fathers," (*1 Peter 1:18, ASV),* "a yoke . . . which neither our fathers nor we were able to bear" (*Acts 15:10).* But God's Ten Commandments are no adversary—they show us our need of Christ! Nullifying the doctrines and traditions of men (*Colossians 2:8, 22)* does not mean that any of God's holy commandments have been nullified.

The "sabbaths" of *Colossians 2:16* are not the holy Sabbath of the fourth commandment. When Paul says that we should not let anyone condemn us with respect to festivals, new moons or sabbaths, he adds "which are a shadow of things to come" (*Colossians 2:16, 17).* This phrase clearly points to the sacrificial system of the old covenant (*Hebrews 8:5; 10:1)* which ended at the cross, as the veil in the temple was torn in two, from top to bottom (*Matthew 27:51).* Added to this is the fact that, whenever the three elements, "holiday [feast], new moon, and Sabbath days," are used in the Old Testament (*1 Chronicles 23:31; 2 Chronicles 2:4; 8:13; 31:3; Ezra 3:5; Nehemiah 10:33; Isaiah 1:13–14; Ezekiel 45:17; 46:3;* and *Hosea 2:11* with certain variations), the passage is emphasizing sacrificial, ceremonial elements. (Note also that *Arndt & Gingrich* give the definition "the Sabbath feasts" as a possible translation for the plural *ta sabbata* in *Isaiah 1:13.*)

The Sabbath of creation is inherently different from the shadowy sacrificial system and is clearly set apart from other Old Testament celebrations (*Leviticus 23:38*). It is suited to *meet current human needs,* as well as to help us remember *God's act of creation* and *His wonderful work of sanctification (Exodus 20:8–11; 31:13).* The fact that many Christians still take a day for rest and worship (albeit the first day) demonstrates that these practical needs did not cease with the death of Christ on the cross.

Q₉ If we keep the Sabbath, aren't we trying to be justified by the law and not by grace?

It is true that it is not our keeping of His commandments that saves us. It is not because we have not killed anyone or because we honor our parents or because we don't worship other gods or because we keep the Sabbath that we stand justified before God. None of these commandments give a person right standing with God, for those who have not outwardly broken the commandments have violated the spirit of the commandments in their hearts (*Matthew 5:28*). Paul declares:

"For all have sinned, and come short of the glory of God."
Romans 3:23.

Neither can we use the commandments to make up for our past sins against God, for, while the law is fully capable of showing us where we have fallen short of God's expectations (*Psalm 19:7*) and of leading us to recognize our need of Christ (*Romans 3:23; 10:4*), it cannot free us from the stranglehold that sin has on our lives through our sinful human nature (*Romans 7:14*) and through the fear of rejection that comes from knowing that we have failed God (*1 John 4:17, 18*).

"And the commandment, which was ordained to life, I found to be unto death.¹¹ For sin, taking occasion by the commandment, deceived me, and by it slew me.¹² Wherefore the law is holy, and the commandment holy, and just, and good.¹³ Was then that which is good made death unto me? God forbid. But sin, that it might appear sin, working death in me by that which is good; that sin by the commandment might become exceeding sinful." Romans 7:10–13.

So, what good are the commandments? They play an important role for human beings. They were ordained to bring life (*Romans 7:10*), to reveal God's will (*Romans 2:18*), to define, point out, and emphasize the degree of our sin (*1 John 3:4; Romans 3:20; 4:15; 1 Corinthians 15:56; Romans 5:20; 7:13*). In other words, the commandments are a needed diagnostic tool for assessing the spiritual condition of those who are out of harmony with God's will and who need to be brought to repentance (*1 Timothy 1:7–9*). Like a spiritual mirror, they play an important role in revealing the true nature of man's moral shortcomings, convicting him of sin and of his need of the One who can change his heart and life (*Psalm 19:7*).

"For if any be a hearer of the word, and not a doer, he is like unto a man beholding his natural face in a glass:²⁴ For he beholdeth himself, and goeth his way, and straightway forgetteth what manner of man he was.²⁵ But whoso looketh into the perfect law of liberty, and continueth therein, he being not a forgetful hearer, but a doer of the work, this man shall be blessed in his deed." James 1:23–25.

In *Romans 7*, Paul illustrates the diagnostic role of the law in terms of his own spiritual experience. If Paul had never heard the tenth commandment of God's law say, "Thou shalt not covet" (*Romans 7:7–8*), he would have remained unaware of the presence of sin in his life. But when the commandment came and spoke to him, revealing his sin, it declared him worthy of death (*Romans 7:9*). Was the law then an instrument of sin? Paul says, no. "The law of God" (*Romans 7:22; 7:25; 8:7*) is "holy" and the commandment that condemned him is "holy, just and good" (*Romans 7:12, 16*). Paul confesses that, in his "inward man," he delights in the law of God. But Paul has a problem. He is by nature *carnal* (*Romans 7:14, 22*) and his carnal nature is disconnected from God and controlled by sin. On the other hand, the law is *spiritual* and can only be kept by one who is *spiritual* (*Romans 2:29; Romans 7:6; 2 Corinthians 3:6*). Paul is out of harmony with the law and with the Lawgiver and powerless to live by the law's high principles. How can Paul's dilemma be resolved?

As we have said, it won't be by the law. For the law is only a diagnostic tool. It is not medicine. It can do nothing to remedy the soul sickness of our human nature (*Romans 8:3*). But what the law could not do, Christ came to earth in human nature to accomplish. Through His life and death, He reconnects or "reconciles" us to God. By His death, Christ broke the power of sin (*Romans 5:10*), demonstrated God's love for us, in spite of our failings (*Romans 13:10*), and won our hearts back to God, forgiving us our sins, giving us eternal life (*John 3:16*), and rescuing us from sin's grasp (*Matthew 1:21*). By His life, Jesus makes us whole, giving us His grace and Spirit to overcome sin in the flesh (*Romans 5:10; 8:3*) and to fulfill the righteousness of the law (*Romans 8:4*). So then, we keep the law *not to be saved*, but because *we have been saved* and because Jesus lives, by His Spirit, in our hearts.

"There is therefore now no condemnation to them which are in Christ Jesus, who walk not after the flesh, but after the Spirit. [2] For the law of the Spirit of life in Christ Jesus hath made me free from the law of sin and death. [3] For what the law could not do, in that it was weak through the flesh, God sending his own Son in the likeness of sinful flesh, and for sin, condemned sin in the flesh: [4] That the righteousness of the law might be fulfilled in us, who walk not after the flesh, but after the Spirit." *Romans 8:1–4.*

Q_{10} Couldn't we *rest* on the Sabbath but *worship* on Sunday?

The idea of separate rest and worship days has recently started to catch on in some circles. Michael Card (the singer/song writer) and Steve Green (singer), for example, *rest* on Sabbath, but *worship* with local congregations on Sunday. But this was not the practice of either Jesus or Paul. They didn't rest on the Sabbath and worship on Sunday (*Luke 4:16*; *Acts 17:2*). We can applaud these men for recognizing the biblical truth of the seventh-day Sabbath rest, but, if we are going to worship the Creator (*Revelation 14:7*), why not do so on the day that He picked out (*Genesis 2:1*)?

Some practical suggestions for observing the Sabbath:

➢ Since it is a day for *physical rest,* put off regular household work for other days (*Exodus 20:9; Mark 2:27*)

➢ Since it is a day for *worship,* put aside the things that distract from communion with God (*Isaiah 58:13; Luke 2:49*)

➢ Since it is a day for *uplifting social interaction,* find a Sabbath-keeping congregation to worship with (*Luke 4:16; Acts 17:2; Hebrews 10:25*)

➢ Since it is a day for *service,* use it to lift the burdens of others by visiting, sharing, helping, and witnessing (*Luke 6:9; 13:15*)

All too often when we get someone a gift, we pick out something that we ourselves would like. But, if we really want to please the other person, wouldn't it be better to find out what he or she would really like? God has not left it a mystery as to which day He prefers, and He promises:

". . . them that honor Me I will honor . . ." 1 Samuel 2:30.

When all other voices are hushed, do you not hear God's voice calling through the Scriptures for you to spend time with Him?

"Come unto me all ye that labor and are heavy laden and I will give you rest." Matthew 11:28.

Putting aside all lesser loyalties, can you not . . .

give God His due by giving God His day?

Sources

Adult *Quarterly,* Southern Baptist Convention series, Aug. 15, 1937.

America, January 4, 1941, vol. 64, p. 343.

Associated Press, "Pope Calls for Moral and Religious Action, Not Just Planning," *Evening Star* (Washington, D.C.), September 8, 1947, p. A-12.

Bacchiocchi, Samuele, *From Sabbath to Sunday* (Rome: The Pontifical Gregorian University Press, 1977), pp. 65, 211, 212.

Bacchiocchi, Samuele, *The Sabbath in Scripture and History* (Washington, D.C.: Review and Herald Publishing Association, 1982), pp. 141, 143, 144.

Bauer, Walter, William F. Arndt, and F. Wilbur Gingrich, *A Greek-English Lexicon of the New Testament and Other Early Christian Literature* (Chicago: The University of Chicago Press, 1957), p. 746.

Binney, Amos and Daniel Steele, *Theological Compend* (New York: The Methodist Book Concern, 1875), p. 171.

Brady, Priest, in an address, reported in the Elizabeth, *New Jersey News,* March 18, 1903.

Brerewood, Edward, *A Learned Treatise of the Sabbath,* Oxford, 1631, p. 77.

Brown, F., S.R. Driver, & C.A. Briggs, *A Hebrew and English Lexicon of the Old Testament* (Oxford University Press, 1951).

Butler, Francis J., *Holy Family Series of Catholic Catechisms* (Boston: Thomas J. Flynn & Co., 1904), p. 63.

Campbell, Alexander, *The Christian Baptist,* February 2, 1824, vol. 1, No. 7.

Carson, D. A., editor, *From Sabbath to Lord's Day* (Grand Rapids, MI: Zondervan, 1982), pp. 135–136, 255.

Carver, William Owen, *Sabbath Observance* (Nashville, TN: Broadman Press, 1940), p. 49.

Catechism of the Catholic Church (New York: Doubleday, 1994), pp. 580, 581, 585.

Catholic Press, Sydney, Australia, August, 1900.

Chalmers, E. M., *How Sunday Came Into the Christian Church,* p. 3.

Church & State, May, 1992, p. 19 (115) and October, 1985.

Clement of Alexandria, *The Ante-Nicene Fathers,* Vol. 2, The Stromata, Or Miscellanies, Book 5, Chapter 14, "Greek Plagiarism From the Hebrews."

Codex Justinianus, lib. 3, tit. 12, 3; trans. in Philip Schaff, *The History of the Christian Church,* vol. 3, p. 380, note 1.

Coleman, Lyman, *Ancient Christianity Exemplified,* chap. 26, sec. 2, p. 527.

Conway, Bertrand L., *The Question-Box Answers* (New York: The Columbus Press, 1910), pp. 254, 255. Issued earlier by "The Missionary Society of St. Paul the Apostle in the State of New York."

Conway, Bertrand L., *The Question Box* (New York: Paulist Press, 1960), p. 410.

Council of Florence, Session XXV (July 6, 1439), Definitio, in Mansi, *Sacrorum Counciliorum,* vol. 31, col. 1031. Latin.

Council of Laodicea, c. A.D. 337, canon 29, quoted in Charles Joseph Hefele, *A History of the Councils of the Church,* vol. 2 (Edinburgh: T. and T. Clark, 1896), p. 316.

Cumont, Franz F. V. M., *Astrology and Religion Among the Greeks and Romans* (reprint: New York: Dover Publications, Inc., 1960), p. 55.

Cumont, Franz F. V. M., "The Frontier Provinces of the East," in *The Cambridge Ancient History,* vol. 11 (Cambridge: Cambridge University Press, 1936), pp. 643, 646–647.

Dale, Dr. Robert William, *The Ten Commandment* (London: Hodder and Stoughton), pp. 100–101.

Davies, W.D., *Christian Origins and Judaism,* n.d., p. 74.

de Ancharano, Petrus, quoted in Lucius Ferraris, *Prompta Bibliotheca,* vol. 6 of 8 (Venice: Caspa Storti, 1772), p. 29 art. 2, "Papa." Latin.

de Fosso, Gaspare [Ricciulli] (Archbishop of Reggio), Address in the 17th session of the Council of Trent (the Council of Trent was convened in response to the Reformation), Jan. 18, 1562, in Mansi, *Sacrorum Counciliorum,* vol. 33, cols. 529, 530. Latin.

de Ségur, Monsignor Louis Gaston, *Plain Talk about the Protestantism of To-day* (Boston: Patrick Donahoe, 1868), p. 225.

di Bruno, Joseph Faà, *Catholic Belief* (New York: Benziger Brothers, 1884), p. 45.

Didache, *The Apostolic Fathers,* edited by J.B. Lightfoot (Grand Rapids: Baker Book House, 1988), p. 221, 232.

Domville, Sir William, *Examination of the Six Texts,* pp. 6, 7 (supplement).

Dowling, John, *History of Romanism,* 13th Edition, p. 65.

Durant, Will, *Caesar and Christ* (New York: Simon and Schuster, 1944), pp. 595, 671, 672.

Dwight, Timothy, *Theology,* sermon 107, 1818 ed., vol. IV, p. 41.

Economist, October 19, 1991, p. 16.

Enright, Priest Thomas, CSSR, President of Redemptorist College, Kansas City, Mo., in a lecture at Hartford, Kansas, February 18, 1884, and the *American Sentinel* (a New York Roman Catholic journal), June 1893, p. 173.

Epiphanius, *The Panarion of Epiphanius of Salamis,* Book 1 (Sects 1–46), translated by Frank Williams (Brill Academic Publishers, 1987), section 29.

Epistle of Barnabas, chap. 16, trans. in A. Roberts and J. Donaldson, editors, *The Ante-Nicene Fathers,* vol. 1, p. 273.

Eusebius, *Church History,* book III, chap. 25, sec. 4. The Nicene and Post-Nicene Fathers, vol. I, p. 156.

Eusebius, *Life of Constantine,* book 1, chapter 28, *The Nicene and Post-Nicene Fathers,* second series, volume 1, translated by Ernest Cushing Richardson, Ph.D., librarian and associate professor in Hartford Theological Seminary.

Eusebius, *Commentary on the Psalms,* on Ps. 91 (92): 2, 3, in J. -P. Migne, *Patrologia Graeca,* Vol. 23, col. 1172.

Evangelicals and Catholics Together: The Christian Mission in the Third Millennium, signed March 29, 1994.

Eyton, Canon Robert, *The Ten Commandments.*

Explanation of the Church Catechism, p. 8.

Fausset, A. R., *Bible Dictionary* (Grand Rapids: Zondervan Publishing House, 1949), p. 666.

Finley, Mark, *The Almost Forgotten Day* (Siloam Springs, AK: The Concerned Group, Inc., 1988), pp. 60-93.

First-Day Observance, pp. 17, 19.

Fisher, George Park, *History of the Christian Church* (New York: Scribner, 1900), p. 118.

Flynn, Ted and Maureen, *The Thunder of Justice* (Sterling, VA: MaxKol Communication, Inc., 1993), p. 30.

Frederick, Rev. William, *Sunday and the Christian Sabbath,* pp. 169, 170 (quoted in *Signs of the Times,* September 6, 1927).

Geiermann, Peter, CSSR, *The Convert's Catechism of Catholic Doctrine,* 1957 edition (St. Louis: B. Herder Book Co., 1910), p. 50.

Gibbon, Edward, *Decline and Fall of the Roman Empire* (New York: American Book Exchange, 1880), vol. 1, chap. 15, p. 387.

Gibbons, James Cardinal, *The Faith of Our Fathers* (originally published 1876, republished TAN Books and Publishers, Inc., copyright 1980), p. 80. (Note: other editions omit the reference to Sunday.)

Gieseler, Johann Karl Ludwig (1793–1854), "Apostolic Age to A.D. 70," *A Text-book of Church History* (New York: Harper and Brothers, 1857–1880), Section 29.

Gildea, William L., "Paschale Gaudium," in *The Catholic World,* 58, March, 1894, p. 809.

Graham, Billy, "My Answer."

Graham, Billy, "The Better Life," *Billy Graham Answers Your Questions* (Minneapolis, MN: World Wide Publications), pp. 45, 46, 51.

Guinness, H. Grattan, *Romanism and the Reformation,* lecture 4, delivered under the auspices of the Protestant Educational Institute, at Exeter Hall, England, spring 1887.

Halsberghe, Gaston H., *The Cult of Sol Invictus,* (Leiden, 1972), p. 26.

Harnack, Adolf von, *History of Dogma* (Boston: Little, Brown, and Company, 1898) vol. I, p. 128, quoted in Benjamin Wilkinson, *Our Authorized Bible Vindicated* (Washington, D.C., 1930), p. 11.

Heggtveit, H. G., *Illustreret Kirkehistorie* (Christiania: Cammermeyers Boghandel, 1891–1895), p. 202.

Heylyn, Dr. Peter, of the Church of England, quoted in *History of the Sabbath,* Part 2, chapter 1, p. 410.

Sources

Hiscox, Dr. E. T., author of *The Baptist Manual*, report of his sermon at the Baptist Minister's Convention, in *New York Examiner*, November 13, 1893. (From a photostatic copy of a notarized statement provided by Dr. Hiscox to the Review & Herald Press.)

Hurlbut, Jesse L., *The Story of the Christian Church* (Philadelphia: John C. Winston Company, 1933), p. 41.

Hyde, Walter Woodburn, *Paganism to Christianity in the Roman Empire* (Philadelphia: University of Pennsylvania Press, 1946), pp. 60, 171, 257, 261.

Justin Martyr, *Dialogue with Trypho, a Jew*, chaps. 16, 21, 24, trans. in A. Roberts and J. Donaldson, editors, *The Ante-Nicene Fathers, vol. 1, p. 390.*

Keenan, Rev. Stephen, *A Doctrinal Catechism* (New York: P J. Kenedy and Sons, 1876), 3rd edition, p. 174.

Kelly, Vincent J., *Forbidden Sunday and Feast-Day Occupations* (Washington: Catholic University of America Press, 1943), pp. 2, 29, 203.

Kennedy, D. James, "The Gift of Rest," *Coral Ridge Hour*, November 4, 2001.

Kennedy, D. James, "Why the Law of God?" *Coral Ridge Hour*, September 9, 2001.

Killen, William D., *The Ancient Church* (New York: Anson D. F. Randolph & Company, 1883), pp. xv, xvi.

Lanaro, John, *Catholic Twin Circle*, August 25, 1985, quoted in *Church and State Magazine*, October 1985.

Latourette, Kenneth Scott, *A History of Christianity* (New York: Harper & Row, 1975), vol. 1, p. 121.

Lewis, Abram Herbert, D.D., "Catholic Proof," *Catholic Mirror*, December 23, 1893 [reprinted in the pamphlet, *Rome's Challenge: Why Do Protestants Keep Sunday?*].

Lindsell, Harold, *Christianity Today*, November 5, 1976.

Lowndes, Jack (of the Lord's Day Alliance), interview in "(Sabbath) A Time to Rest," ReligionToday.com, August 12, 1999.

Lucas, Dr. D. H., in *The Christian Oracle*, January 23, 1890.

Martin, Malachi, *The Keys of This Blood*, 1990, pp. 15, 492, 657.

Martin, Walter, *The Kingdom of the Cults*, 1997 (Bloomington, MN: Bethany House Publishers), pp. 460ff.

McClintock and Strong, *Cyclopedia of Biblical Theological and Ecclesiastical Literature*, vol. 9, p. 196.

Melady, Thomas Patrick, *The Ambassador's Story—The United States and the Vatican in World Affairs* (Huntington, Ind.: Our Sunday Visitor Pub. Division, 1994), p. 10, 178.

Ministry, December 1979.

Moody, Dwight L., *Weighed and Wanting* (Chicago: Revell, 1898), pp. 46–47.

Morer, T. M., *Dialogues on the Lord's Day* (London, 1701), p. 23.

Mosheim, Rev. John Lawrence, *Ecclesiastical History* (Modesto, CA: H.J. Boyd, 1849) book 1, cent. 2, part 2, chap. 3, sec. 7, quoted in E.J. Waggoner, *Fathers of the Catholic Church* (Oakland, CA: Pacific Press Publishing Company, 1888), p. 63 and cent. 2, part 2, chap. 4, par. 5, quoted in Alonzo T. Jones, *The Great Empires of Prophecy from Babylon to the Fall of Rome*, p. 381.

Mosheim, Rev. John Lawrence, *Historical Commentaries*, Century 1, sec. 53, quoted in John N. Andrews, *History of the Sabbath*, sec. 2, chapter iv, p. 234.

Mosna, Corrado S., *Storia della Domenica dalle origini fino agli Inizi del V Secolo*, 1969 (Rome, Italy), pp. 354, 366–367.

Moulton, Harold K., *The Analytical Greek Lexicon* (Grand Rapids: Zondervan, 1978), p. 361.

Mueller, John Theodore, *Sabbath or Sunday*, pp. 15, 16.

National & International Religion Report, Feb. 11, 1991 [sited in G. Edward Reid, *Even at the Door* (Hagerstown, MD: Review & Herald, 1994), p. 69].

Neander, Augustus, *The History of the Christian Religion and Church*, trans. by Henry John Rose (Philadelphia: James M. Campbell & Co., 1843), p. 186. (Note: later translations omit statement about Sunday.)

Newman, John Henry Cardinal, *An Essay on the Development of Christian Doctrine* (London: Longmans, Green, and Co., 1906), p. 373.

Our Sunday Visitor, February 5, 1950.

Ostling, Richard N., "A Refinement of Evil," *TIME*, October 4, 1993.

Phillips, David (director of the Church Society, Church of England), "Pope launches crusade to save Sunday," World News, *The Sunday Times*, July 5, 1998.

Philo, translated by C.D. Yonge, *The Works of Philo* (Peabody, MA: Hendrickson Publishers, 1993), p. 13.

Piroutek, Erin, *The Observer,* University Wire, South Bend, Indiana, November 1, 1999.

Pope John Paul II, May 31, 1998, *Dies Domini ("The Lord's Day").*

Pope John Paul II, *Make Room for the Mystery of God*, pp. 7–9 (quoted in *Sunday's Coming*, p. 60).

Pope John Paul II, *Catholic News Service, Oct.* 9, 1995.

Pope Leo XIII, Encyclical Letter "The Reunion of Christendom," dated June 20, 1894, trans. in *The Great Encyclical Letters of Pope Leo XIII* (New York: Benziger, 1903), p. 304.

Pope Pius XII, in his encyclical letter, "The Mystical Body of Christ," June 29, 1943.

Pope Sylvester, quoted by S. R. E. Humbert, *Adversus Graecorum Calumnias*, in J. -P. Migne, *Patrologia Graeca,* p. 143.

Postema, Don, *Catch Your Breath: God's Invitation to Sabbath Rest*, (CRC [Christian Reformed Church] Publications, August 1997), pp. 5, 15.

Report of Joint Anglican-Roman Catholic International Commission, May 1999.

Ringgold, James T., *The Law of Sunday*, p. 267.

Robertson, Pat, audiotape in a series on the Ten Commandments, "A Day Made for You."

Robertson, Pat, *Christian American,* October 1993.

Robertson, *The New World Order*

Robertson, "Is Saturday or Sunday the True Sabbath?" *Christian Broadcasting Network.*

Robinson, James Harvey, *Introduction to the History of Western Europe,* p. 30.

Rordorf, Willy, *Sunday* (Philadelphia: Westminister Press, 1968), p. 157.

Sentinel (a newsletter published by Saint Catherine Catholic Church of Algonac, Michigan), May 21, 1995.

Seymour, Bishop, *Why We Keep Sunday.*

Socrates Scholasticus, *Ecclesiastical History,* Book 5, chap. 22, trans. in *Nicene and Post-Nicene Fathers,* 2d series, vol. 2, p. 132.

Schuller, Dr. Robert, *Los Angeles Herald Examiner,* September 19, 1987.

Shea, John Gilmary, "The Observance of Sunday and Civil Laws for Its Enforcement," *The American Catholic Quarterly Review,* 8 (Philadelphia: January, 1883), pp. 139, 152.

Smith, Albert, Chancellor of the Archdiocese of Baltimore, replying for the Cardinal in a letter dated February 10, 1920.

Smith, Hugh, *History of the Christian Church,* pp. 50, 51, 69.

Sozomen, Hermias, *Ecclesiastical History,* bk. 7, chap. 19, trans. in *Nicene and Post-Nicene Fathers,* 2nd Series, vol. 2, p. 390.

Sverdrup, George, "En ny Dag" ("A New Day"), in "Sondagen og dens Helligholdelse" ("Sunday and Its Observance"), reprinted from *Kvartal-Skrift (Quarterly Journal),* 4 (1878), 5 (1879), in his *Samlede Skrifter (Collected Works)*, ed. by Andreas Helland, vol. 1 (Minneapolis: Frikirkens Boghandels Forlag, 1909), p. 342. Norwegian.

Stanley, Dean Arthur Penrhyn, *Lectures on the History of the Eastern Church* (New York: Charles Scribner, 1884), Lecture 6, p. 184.

Strand, Kenneth A., *Kenneth A., The Sabbath in Scripture and History* (Washington, D.C.: Review and Herald Publishing Association, 1982), pp. 141, 143, 144, 323, 324, 346–350.

Studies in the Lectionary Text of the Greek New Testament, 1944, II, sec. 3, p. 12.

Taylor, Bishop Joseph Jeremy, *The Rule of Conscience* (London: Longman, Brown, Green, and Longmans, 1851), pp. 456, 457.

Taylor, Bishop Joseph Judson, *The Sabbath Question* (New York: Fleming H. Revell Co., 1914), pp. 16, 41.

The Associated Press, December 11, 1984 and February 17, 1987.

The Augsburg Confession (1530), part 2, art. 7, "Of Ecclesiastical Power," trans. in Phillip Schaff, *The Creeds of Christendom* (New York: Harper, 1919), vol. 3, p. 64.

The Bakersfield Californian, August 27, 1989.

The Catholic Encyclopedia, 1910 edition, vol. 7, p. 796.

The Catholic Encyclopedia, 1911 edition, vol. 14, p. 765.

The Catholic National, July, 1, 1895.

The Catholic Record of London, Ontario, Canada, September 1, 1923.

The Catholic World, June 1871, pp. 422, 423 and August 1871, p. 589.

The Catholic World, August 1877, p. 620.

The Christian Sabbath (2d ed.; Baltimore: The Catholic Mirror, 1893), p. 29.

The Courier, Findlay, Ohio, March 29, 1988.

Sources

The Dallas Morning News, October 1, 1989.

The Fathers of the Church: Writings of Saint Justin Martyr (Washington, D.C.: The Catholic University of America Press), p. 17.

The Herald, Sydney, Australia, March 30, 1982.

The Montgomery Advertiser, September 12, 1987.

"The Question Box," The Catholic Universe Bulletin, 69 (Aug. 14, 1942), p. 4.

The Sunday Problem (Philadelphia: The United Lutheran Publication House, 1923), p. 36.

Thomas, H. F., chancellor for James Cardinal Gibbons, November 11, 1895.

TIME, November 10, 1986.

"To Tell You the Truth," The Catholic Virginian, vol. 22 (Oct. 3, 1947), no. 49.

Tuberville, Priest Henry, An Abridgement of the Christian Doctrine, p. 58.

Vyhmeister, Werner K. "The Sabbath in Asia," The Sabbath in Scripture and History (Washington, D.C.: Review & Herald), 1982, p. 151.

Vine, W.E., Vine's Complete Expository Dictionary of Old and New Testament Words (New York: Thomas Nelson / Word, 1985).

Webster, Hutton, Rest Days (New York: The Macmillan Company, 1916), p. 270.

Wehr, Jeff, Our Firm Foundation, April 1996, p. 4.

Wesley, John, Sermons on Several Occasions, vol. 1, no. 25.

Wharey, James, Sketches of Church History (Presbyterian Board of Publications, 1840), p. 23.

White, Ellen G. The Great Controversy (Mountain View, CA: Pacific Press Publishing Association, 1939) pp. 563, 573.

Williams, Isaac, Plain Sermons On The Catechism, vol. 1, pp. 334, 336.

Illustration credits

cover "Rest," *Honor Him Ministries*

vi America, It's Time to Give God Time, *Honor Him Ministries*

8 John Wesley, courtesy *United Methodist Church*; D. James Kennedy, *Coral Ridge Hour* website; Billy Graham, *internet graphic;*

10 Pat Robertson, *internet graphic*

11 finger of God writing commandments, *LLT Productions*

14 Tony Evans, *internet graphic*

24 Alexander Campbell, *internet graphic;* Change of the law, *Honor Him Ministries*

28 Sun, *clipart*

29 Justin Martyr, *Honor Him Ministries*

32 library of Alexandria, *LLT Productions;* papal palace of Rome, *LLT Productions;*

33 8th day Sunday, *Honor Him Ministries*

34 Resurrected Lord, *clip art*

36 Constantine, *Honor Him Ministries*

41 Ruins of temple in Pella, *LLT Productions*

44 Samuele Bacchiocchi, back cover of *The Sabbath Under Crossfire*

48 Sol, sun god of Mithraism, *Honor Him Ministries*

49 *Fides* over the pulpit of the Benedictine Melk Monastery on the Danube in Austria, built in the early 1900's. In FIDES' left hand is a golden cup (in front of the cross), and behind her right shoulder is a pagan sunburst image, from a photo by Artephot, Paris (Nimatallah) *LLT Productions;* "La Verita" with solar blaze, from video *Israel of the Alps* (c) 1993 *LLT Productions.*

50 Cardinal Newman, *internet graphics*

51 Constantine's vision of cross above the sun, *Honor Him Ministries*

55 James Cardinal Gibbons, *Grolier Multimedia Encyclopedia,* 1997 edition

58 Martin Luther, *internet graphic*

61 homage to Pope, *LLT Productions*

62 Pope Pius XII, *internet graphic*

63 Pope Leo XIII, *clipart*

64 Malachi Martin, back cover *The Keys of this Blood*

66 Pope and Dalai Lama, *LLT Productions*

68 Evangelicals & Catholics, *Adventist Review,* April 28, 1994; cover *Evangelicals & Catholics Together: Toward a Common Mission,* by Charles Colson and Richard John Neuhaus

69 Pope and image of Mary, *LLT Productions*

70 Jesus, our high priest, *Honor Him Ministries;* "A Half-Millennium Rift," *TIME,* July 6, 1998, p. 80

71 Dr. Robert Schuller, *Hour of Power*

72 cover *Catechism of the Catholic Church*

73 cover *The Thunder of Justice* (Sterling, VA: MaxKol Communications, 1993) by Ted and Maureen Flynn; cover *The New World Order* (Dallas: Word Publishing, 1991) by Pat Robertson

76 Open Bible, *clipart*

83 Jesus in upper room, *Honor Him Ministries*

85 John in vision *Honor Him Ministries*

94 gift, *Honor Him Ministries*

101 covers *From Sabbath to Sunday; The Sabbath Under Crossfire; The (New, Illustrated) Great Controversy; Truth Left Behind; Trials and Triumph*

back photo Pastor Kevin Morgan, *Honor Him Ministries.*

For further study

*T*wo very important works on the Sabbath are Dr. Samuele Bacchiocchi's books, *From Sabbath to Sunday* and *The Sabbath Under Crossfire*. They are available from the author by phone, (616) 471–2915, or via his web page:

http://www2.andrews.edu/~samuele/books

The (New, Illustrated) Great Controversy, tells the dramatic story (with 450 color photos) of God's faithful people from the time of the destruction of Jerusalem to their ultimate victory, described in the book of Revelation. It is available by phone: 1-800-558-4478, or via the *LLT Productions* web page:

http://www.tagnet.org/llt

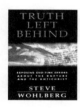

Steve Wohlberg has written several *must-read* books on biblical prophecy. In *Truth Left Behind*, he takes a careful, insightful look at Revelation's final prophecies about the Rapture, the Tribulation, the Antichrist and his deadly mark (*Revelation 14:9, 14*). This and his other books are available through his website:

http://www.truthleftbehind.com

In Crystal Earnhardt's *Trials and Triumph*, you will be inspired by the stories of those whom God blessed when they have stepped out in faith to keep His holy Sabbath. (It also includes practical help for those with Sabbath work conflicts.) It is available through the *Amazing Facts* website:

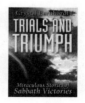

http://www.amazingfacts.com

We'd love to send you a free catalog of titles we publish
or even hear your thoughts, reactions, criticism,
about things you did or didn't like about this
or any other book we publish.

Just write or call us at:

TEACH Services, Inc.
Brushton, New York 12916-9738
1-800/367-1998

www.tsibooks.com